William H. G. Kingston

Ned Garth

Or, Made Prisoner in Africa

William H. G. Kingston

Ned Garth
Or, Made Prisoner in Africa

ISBN/EAN: 9783337130565

Printed in Europe, USA, Canada, Australia, Japan

Cover: Foto ©ninafisch / pixelio.de

More available books at **www.hansebooks.com**

NED GARTH;

OR,

MADE PRISONER IN AFRICA.

A Tale of the Slave Trade.

BY

WILLIAM H. G. KINGSTON,

Author of " *Sunshine Bill,*" " *Michael Penguyne,*" " *Owen Hartley,*"
&c., &c., &c.

PUBLISHED UNDER THE DIRECTION OF THE
COMMITTEE OF GENERAL LITERATURE AND EDUCATION,
APPOINTED BY THE SOCIETY FOR PROMOTING
CHRISTIAN KNOWLEDGE.

LONDON:

SOCIETY FOR PROMOTING CHRISTIAN KNOWLEDGE,
NORTHUMBERLAND AVENUE, W.C.; 43, QUEEN VICTORIA STREET, E.C.
BRIGHTON: 129, NORTH STREET.
NEW YORK: E. & J. B. YOUNG & CO.

"He continued firing away as fast as the gun could be run in and loaded."

"'Stop that youngster!' exclaimed Rhymer."

"The monster staggered on, and was about to seize the Arab with its trunk, when, uttering a shriek of pain and baffled rage, down it came with a crash to the earth."

NED GARTH;

OR,

Made Prisoner in Africa.

CHAPTER I.

"AN you make her out, Ned? My eyes are not so sharp as they used to be, and I lost sight of the craft when the squall came on."

"She has tacked, uncle; I see her masts in one, and she's standing to the westward."

"I was afraid so; she must be a stranger, or she would have kept her course. She'll not weather the head as she's now standing, and if it doesn't clear and show her the land, she'll be on shore, as sure as my name is John Pack."

▲

The speaker was a strongly built man, dressed in a thick pea-coat buttoned closely over his breast, the collar turned up to protect his neck. A white, low-crowned, weather-beaten, broadish-brimmed hat covered his head, and he held in his hand a thick stick, which he pressed firmly on the ground as he walked, for he had been deprived of one of his legs, its place being supplied by a wooden substitute resembling a mop handle in shape. His appearance was decidedly nautical, and though-habited in plain clothes, he might have been known at a glance to be a naval officer.

His companion, a boy of about fourteen years of age, though from his height and breadth of shoulders he might have been supposed to be older, wore a thick monkey jacket, a necessary protection against the strong wind and dense masses of rain and mist which swept up from the ocean.

They stood on the top of a cliff on the southern coast of England, which, circling round from the north-west to the south-east, formed a broad deep bay, terminated on the further side by a bluff headland, and on the other by a rocky point, a ledge partly under water extending beyond it.

The bay was indeed a dangerous place to enter with so heavy a gale from the south-west as was now blowing.

Lieutenant Pack and his young nephew Edward Garth were returning home from an errand of mercy to an old fisherman who had been severely injured by

the upsetting of his boat, in a vain endeavour to go off
to a coaster in distress, which foundered in sight of
land, when he was washed on shore amid the fragments
of his boat, narrowly escaping with his life. Although
the fisherman's cottage was upwards of two miles off, the
old lieutenant trudged daily over to see him, and on
this occasion had been accompanied by his nephew,
carrying a basket containing certain delicacies prepared
by the kind hands of Miss Sarah Pack, or sister
Sally, as he was wont to call her. He and his
nephew had started later than usual, and the gloom of
an autumn evening had overtaken them when they
were still some distance from home. He had caught
sight of the vessel, apparently a large brig, and had
at once perceived her dangerous position.

For some time he and his nephew stood watching
the stranger from the cliff.

" Here she comes again ! " cried Ned.

" She made out the land sooner than I expected she
would," observed the lieutenant ; " but she'll scarcely
weather the point even now, unless the wind shifts.
She can't do it—she can't do it ! " he cried, striking
the ground in his eagerness with his stick. " Run on,
Ned, to the coast-guard station. If you meet one of
the men, tell him, in case he hasn't seen her, that I
think the vessel will be on shore before long. But if
you fall in with no one, go and let Lieutenant Hanson
know what I say, and he'll get his rockets ready, so as
to be prepared to assist the crew whenever the vessel

may strike. Take care, Ned, though, not to fall over the cliff—keep well away from it. On a dark night you cannot see the path clearly, and in many spots, remember, it ends abruptly in places where it wouldn't do to tumble down. I cannot spare you, my boy."

While the lieutenant was shouting out these latter sentences, Edward, eager to obey his uncle's directions, had got to a considerable distance; he, however, very soon came back.

" I met one of the men, uncle," he said, " and he went on to the station faster than I could in the dark, as he knows the short cuts."

" Come along then, we 'll keep an eye on the brig as we walk homeward," said the lieutenant. " I pray that after all she may claw off the land, although she will have a hard job to do it."

The old officer and the boy proceeded on the way they had previously been pursuing. They had gone some distance when they saw a light approaching them.

" Now, if my sister Sally hasn't sent Tom to look for us, or I am much mistaken," he exclaimed to himself rather than to his companion. " Poor soul! she 's been in a precious quandary at our not returning sooner, and has been fancying that we shall be melted by the rain, or carried off the cliffs by the wind, though it blows directly on them."

The lieutenant was right in his conjectures; in another minute a voice was heard shouting, " Dat you, Massa Pack an' Massa Ned ?"

"Aye, aye," answered the lieutenant; "keep your lantern shaded from the sea, or it may be mistaken for a signal."

Directly afterwards a tall figure could be discerned coming towards him. "Missie Sarah in drea'ful way, cos you an' Massa Ned not come back when de wind an' rain kick up such a hulabaloo," said the same voice which had before spoken.

The lieutenant explained the cause of their delay, and bade Tom hasten back and tell his mistress that they would soon be at home, but were anxious to ascertain the fate of a vessel they had discovered closer in shore than she should be. "Beg her not to be alarmed; and, Tom, you come back with a coil of rope and a couple of oars from the boat-house. We may not want them, for I hope the coast-guard men will be up to the spot in time to help, should the craft unfortunately come ashore, but it is just as well to be prepared to render assistance in case of need."

Tom, handing the lantern to the boy, hurried back to execute the orders he had received, the lieutenant and his young companion following at a slower pace. The fast increasing darkness had now completely shut out the brig from sight. When last perceived, however, her head was pointed in a direction which, could she maintain, she might weather the rocks under her lee. Presently the loud report of a gun was heard sounding high above the roar of the seas which broke on the shore.

"That was fearfully near," observed Edward.

"It was indeed," said the lieutenant. "I hope that it will hurry Hanson and his men. The master of the brig has discovered his danger. There is no chance of her escaping, I fear."

"I can see her!" cried the boy; "one of her top-masts has gone, she's drifting bodily on shore."

"Poor fellows! with a heavy sea beating on it; unless she's a stout craft, she'll knock to pieces in a few minutes," observed the lieutenant. "We'll go down to the beach and try what help we can render."

A zig-zag pathway, well known to both of them, led downwards through an opening in the cliff, a short distance from the spot they had reached. The lieutenant and his nephew followed it without hesitation, the former leading and feeling the way with his stick, for it required care to avoid slipping over, and an ugly fall might have been the consequence of a false step. They reached the bottom, however, in safety; and as they hurried along the shingly beach, straining their eyes to discover the whereabouts of the hapless brig, another and another gun was heard, the loud reports rapidly succeeding the bright flashes, showing the nearness of the vessel. The whistling of the wind and the roaring of the waves overpowered all other sounds. They listened for another gun, but listened in vain.

"I feared it would be so," exclaimed the lieutenant; "she must have struck already."

"Yes, yes, I see a dark mass surrounded by foam; that must be her, and not fifty yards off," cried Ned.

As he spoke he could distinguish, in imagination at all events, amid the wild foaming waters, the crash of timbers, and hear the cries of the hapless crew imploring assistance. For an instant, too, he fancied that he saw a smaller object floating on the snowy crests of the waves, but before he could be certain that it was what he supposed, it had disappeared.

"Would that the men with their rockets were here. What can have delayed them? If they don't come soon, not a soul of the crew will be left alive," exclaimed the lieutenant.

Just then a voice hailed, and Edward shouted in return. A dark figure could be seen at the top of the cliff. It was Tom, who rapidly made his way down to where they stood, carrying a pair of oars and a coil of rope.

"The brig is driving in," cried Edward. "She's much nearer than when I first saw her."

"You're right," answered the lieutenant. "In spite of my timber leg, few men could once beat me at swimming; even now I've a mind to go off to the wreck. I might be in time to save some of the people. Here, Tom, hand me the end of the rope, and I'll make it fast round my waist, and do you and Ned pay it out, and haul in again when I shout to you."

"Don't think of going," said Edward; "you have

been ill lately, and are not as strong as you were.
Let me try. I can swim like a fish; you have often
seen me in rough water as well as in smooth. It
won't matter to any one if I am drowned."

"Won't it though! What would Aunt Sally say
if I was to go back without you, Ned?" exclaimed
the lieutenant. "I should never be able to look her
in the face again."

"But I'll do my best not to come to harm," said
Edward; "and you can haul me back if I cannot
make my way through the breakers."

"Let me go, massa," cried Tom, rapidly throwing
off his clothes, and beginning, without further ado, to
fasten the rope round his own waist. "Jis see him tight
—not a slip-knot, massa. Tom Baraka swim tro' worse
seas dan dis on coast ob Africa, as you know. Stick
de oar in de sand. Tie de rope to it, Massa Pack;
you pay out, and off him go."

And before the lieutenant or Ned had time to
speak another word, the black had plunged into the
foaming seas, dragging out the rope which the lieutenant quickly uncoiled. His dark head and back could
be distinguished amid the surging foam, as he made
his way through the breakers for some distance, when
a huge wave rolling in beat him back almost to the
beach. The lieutenant hauled in the rope, fearing
that Tom's legs might be entangled, but the brave
black again sprang forward. He had, however,
another danger besides the sea to encounter. Already

broken spars, planks, and masses of timber, with bales of all sorts, were being hurled on shore, and a blow from some heavy piece of wreck might in an instant disable him. It seemed useless indeed to proceed further; not a human being was likely to have remained alive on the shattered wreck. Probably the larger number were drowned when the boat was upset. Another sea, still fiercer than the former, rushing on with a loud roar, again drove Tom back.

"We must haul in the rope," cried the lieutenant. "I cannot let the brave fellow further risk his life."

But once more it was found that Tom was dragging out the rope.

"I heard a cry, and I fancy I see some one not far from Tom," exclaimed Edward. "Yes, yes! he is making towards the man. Ah, I fear he has missed him; no, he has hold of him. Haul away, uncle, haul away; let me go and help him, there's rope enough to spare," and Ned, securing the slack end of the rope under his arms and seizing the spare oar, dashed forward in time to grasp the man just as the black, exhausted by his exertions, was on the point of letting him go. Another wave breaking at the moment, and hissing as it rushed back in a sheet of foam over the beach, would have swept away the almost rescued man, but Edward, planting his oar deep in the sand, held on while the lieutenant was engaged in hauling Tom out of danger, hastening, the moment he had done so, to assist his nephew in landing the stranger. The latter still breathed, and attempted to raise himself from the sand, though unable to speak.

"You attend to him, Ned, while I look after Tom," said the lieutenant.

The black, however, required no assistance. He proposed, indeed, to again swim off on the chance of finding some other human being struggling for life; but this the lieutenant would not allow. Already the breakers were covered with masses of wreck, amid which not a single person could be seen, though they looked out eagerly, Tom pressing into the seething foam as far as he dared venture, while the lieutenant held up the lantern as a signal to any strong swimmer who might successfully have buffeted with the waves; but he did so with little hope of success. Every now and then he looked round, uttering an exclamation of regret at the non-appearance of the coast-guard, though, had they arrived, it was evident that they would be too late to be of use.

The sea continued to cast up fragments of wreck and cargo on the beach, but the lieutenant and Tom searched in vain for any of their fellow-creatures to whom they might render assistance.

"No use waiting longer, I fear," shouted the lieutenant. "I'll go and look after the man we have saved; the sooner we get him under shelter the better, or he'll be perishing of cold."

" Me stop just a little longer," answered the black.

" Take care though that the sea doesn't carry you off, Tom," cried the lieutenant, even now trusting that some-one else might be rescued.

On returning to the spot where Edward was tending the stranger, he bent down by the side of the latter and felt his heart. "He is still evidently in a very exhausted condition," he observed, holding up his lantern so that the light fell on the man's countenance. "Poor fellow, he does not look as if he were accustomed to a seaman's life."

"I have been rubbing his hands and chest, uncle, and trying what I could do to revive him," said Edward. "We should get him home at once, I am sure."

" Just what I was saying; we must not risk his life on the chance of saving that of others," replied the lieutenant. " Come, Tom," he shouted, " it is of no use, we must carry home this poor fellow; and may be before we get far the coast-guard will be down here and take our places."

At that instant a hail was heard. The lieutenant shouted in return. In a few minutes a party of coast-guard men appeared, headed by their lieutenant, who had heard the guns, and had been searching for the spot where the vessel had struck. The man to whom Edward had given the message had, however, not appeared, having, as was afterwards discovered, fallen over the cliff and nearly lost his life. Lieutenant Hanson said that he would remain on the spot, though his rockets would be useless, as not a man could be clinging to the wreck.

" Let me have one of your people to assist in carrying this poor fellow to my cottage then," said Lieutenant Pack ; " it is more than Tom and I can accomplish, seeing that my timber toe is apt to stick in the soft sand as I trudge along."

" With all my heart," was the answer. " You shall have two, only send them back without delay."

No further time was lost. The coast-guard men, wrapping the stranger in their dry coats, lifted him on their shoulders, Ned and Tom taking his feet, while the lieutenant led the way, lantern in hand, towards his home.

Although a bright light beaming forth from the sitting-room of the lieutenant's abode could alone be distinguished as the party approached, it may be as well to describe it at once. Triton Cottage, as he called it, from the name of the ship on board which he first went to sea, stood on the side of a broad gap or opening in the cliff, some little distance up from the beach, the ground around it being sufficiently level to allow of a fair-sized garden and shrubbery. It was a building of somewhat curious appearance, having no pretentions to what is considered architectural beauty. The lieutenant, notwithstanding, was proud of it, as the larger portion had been erected by his own hands from time to time as he considered it necessary to increase its size, in order to afford sufficient accom-

modation to its inmates, and to obtain a spare room in
which he could put up an old shipmate, or any other
visitor to whom his hospitable feelings might prompt
him to give an invitation. The original building had
been a fisherman's cottage, to which he had added
another story, with a broad verandah in front, while on
either side wings had been attached, the upper portions
composed of wood obtained from wrecks, the bulkheads
serving as wainscoting to the rooms. Both from
their size and the fittings they resembled the cabins of
a small vessel, being warmed also by ship's stoves, with
high flues, curiously topped, rising above the roof,
exhibiting a variety of contrivances to prevent the
smoke from beating down. The tar-bucket and
paint-pot had been brought largely into requisition,
the wood-work of the lower story being covered with a
shining coat of black, while various colours adorned
the walls both inside and out. The old lieutenant might
frequently have been seen, brush in hand, adorning his
mansion, and stopping up every crevice, so as to defy
damp, or rain driven against it by the fiercest of
south-westerly gales. It was substantially roofed
with thick slabs of slate, obtained from a neighbouring
quarry, calculated to withstand the storms of winter
or the thickest downfall of snow. The building
had, however, so slight an appearance that it looked as
if it might be carried by a strong wind into the sea ;
but a closer inspection showed that the materials of
which it was composed were well seasoned and firmly

put together, and though gaily bedecked, fire was the
only element it had to fear, and against that the owner
had taken all necessary precautions.

"Sally, sister Sally!" he shouted, as he neared
the door, "I have brought a guest who requires careful looking after, or he'll slip through our fingers, for
he's pretty well gone already."

As he spoke, the door opened, and a female appeared
holding a shaded lamp in her hand, which the wind
threatened every instant to extinguish. Her figure
was short and slight, her dress a grey silk gown, a
plain lace cap confining her once dark hair, already
sprinkled with grey, drawn back from her forehead,
on which not a wrinkle could be seen. A kind
expression beamed from her countenance, which, if it
had never possessed much beauty, must always have
been pleasant to look upon.

"Thank Heaven you've come back at last, John!
Tom frightened me by the intelligence that a wreck
was on shore, and I knew that you would be exposing
yourself to danger. Have many of the poor fellows
been saved?"

"Only one, I fear," answered the lieutenant,
pointing to the men who now approached. "Take
him into my room, Tom; the sooner he is in bed the
better, and mine is ready for him. Get some warm
broth or a cup of tea made in the meantime. He is
terribly exhausted, and probably has not tasted food
for many hours."

The lieutenant made these remarks as Ned and Tom, with the coast-guard men, conveyed the stranger into the room, when, speedily taking off his wet garments, they placed him in bed.

" By his dress I suspect he is a gentleman," observed the lieutenant to his nephew, as Tom gathered up his wet clothes. "Hand me his watch and purse—it is a heavy one—and that pocket-book. Here is a small case too, something of value probably. He will be glad to know that his property is safe when he comes to. Run and see if the tea is ready. I will get him, if I can, to take a little hot liquid. Tell your aunt and Jane to stir up the fire and get the broth boiling; that will soon set him on his legs I hope."

The lieutenant now managed to pour the warm tea down the throat of the stranger, who opened his eyes, and looking about with an astonished gaze murmured, "Thank you, thank you! Where am I?"

"All right and safe on shore, though you may take my room to be a ship's cabin," answered the lieutenant. "We have got your property, in case you are anxious about it; and after you have had a basin of broth I would advise you to try and go to sleep. It will restore your strength faster than any food we can give you."

The stranger again murmured his thanks, and soon after the broth was brought, following his host's advice, he fell into a quiet slumber.

"He'll require a visit from the doctor perhaps,

though I hope that he'll do well enough now," observed the lieutenant, as he sat at supper with his sister and Ned that evening after he had paid all the attention necessary to his guest.

"I wonder who he can be?" observed Miss Sarah. "You say he was dressed as a gentleman, and has a considerable amount of property in his possession."

"Your female curiosity will probably be gratified to-morrow, when he is able to give an account of himself," replied the lieutenant; "but it matters very little as far as we are concerned. I suspect he'll thank us for doing what it was our simple duty to do, and after he has gone his way we shall probably hear no more of him. Had he been a seaman, without a copper in his pocket, we should have treated him in the same fashion I hope. Remember, Ned, the meaning of having no respect for persons. It is not that we are not to respect those above us, but that we are to treat our fellow-creatures alike, without expectation of reward, and to pull a drowning man, whether a lord or an ordinary seaman, out of the water when we can."

CHAPTER II.

THE next morning Ned went off to summon the doctor from the neighbouring town, for their guest still remained in an apparently dangerous state. Several days passed before he was able to rise. He was evidently, from his conversation and manners, a man of education; but he did not speak of himself, except to mention that his name was Farrance, and that he was on a voyage from the Mediterranean in the " Champion " brig, when she had been cast away; and he again also expressed his gratitude to Miss Sarah Pack for the kindness he was receiving, and to the lieutenant and his companions for preserving his life. He made minute inquiries as to the occurrence, he only remembering that he was clinging to a portion of the wreck after she had struck, when he felt himself washed into the foaming breakers. He appeared to be interested in Ned, whom he drew into conversation, inquiring particularly what profession he intended to follow.

"I wish to enter the navy, as my father and uncle did," answered Ned; "but my uncle says that he has no interest, and that I should have little chance of promotion. Indeed, his means are so limited that I cannot ask him to provide the necessary funds, so I conclude I shall have to go into the merchant service."

"Well, well, you are right in desiring not to be an expense to your uncle. Every man should endeavour, as far as he can, to depend upon his own exertions; however, you have still some time to think about the matter, and you will, I hope, succeed in whatever profession you follow," remarked the stranger.

There was another inmate of the house who appeared to interest him even more than Edward. A little girl of some ten or twelve years of age—a fair-haired, blue-eyed damsel, with a sweet, gentle expression of countenance, yet full of life and spirits. Edward had told him that she was not his sister, although he loved her as much as if she were. The first evening he came into the sitting-room the lieutenant heard him ask her name.

"I am called Mary," she answered; "Uncle John gave me my name when he first found me."

She shortly afterwards left the room. The stranger watched her as she went out with a look of much surprise.

"You may be curious to know the meaning of her remark," observed Miss Sarah. "My brother will tell you how she came into our possession; and very thankful I have been to have so sprightly an.! sweet a young creature under our roof, though at first I confess I felt somewhat anxious when he placed her in my charge."

Mr. Farrance turned an inquiring glance towards his host.

"I have but a short yarn to spin about the matter," said the lieutenant. "Some few years ago, after I had quitted the service, an old friend offered me the command of a ship bound on a voyage round the Cape of Good Hope and up the Red Sea. I was not sorry to obtain employment, and was glad to have the opportunity of making a few pounds, which might assist to keep the pot boiling at home, and help Sally in her housekeeping. Having touched at the Cape, I was steering for Aden, when we were overtaken by a heavy gale, which pretty severely tried my stout ship. We were about to make sail in the morning, the wind having abated and the sea gone down, when an object was seen floating a short distance ahead. On getting nearer, we saw that it was a piece of wreck with a man upon it. Standing on, I hove the ship to, and having lowered a boat, watched with interest her approach to the raft. The man was, I made out, a black. He was holding what looked like a bundle of clothes with one hand, keeping it above the water, which still nearly washed over him. His bundle contained, I had no doubt, something of value, or he would not

have exerted himself as he was doing to preserve it
from the sea. It was of value, and, to my mind, the
most valuable thing in creation—a young child, as I
discovered when the boat returned with the rescued
man, who still held fast to his treasure. We lifted
them both carefully on board. The black sank
exhausted on the deck, making signs to us, however,
to take care of the child. We thought that it was
his own, but when we got a look at its countenance,
greatly to our surprise we found that it was as fair
as any European. How the man had managed to
preserve it during the heavy sea which had been
running for some hours seemed a miracle. We
carried them both into my cabin. The little girl,
you may be sure, had plenty of nurses. She looked
frightened enough at seeing us, but appeared wonderfully little the worse for the exposure to which she
had been subjected ; indeed, although the shawl which
had wrapped her was wet, the water was warm and
the black must have contrived to keep her head well
out of the sea, as her face and hair were only moistened
by the spray.

" Though she seemed almost too young to speak, she
uttered several words in a lingo none of us understood.
In a very short time after we had given her some
food, and she had had a quiet sleep, she seemed more
happy and smiled, and lifted up her face to kiss me
when I bent over her. I thanked Heaven that I had
been the means of saving the little darling.

"It was not until evening that the black, who was pretty well exhausted by his exertions, awoke. I was disappointed, I can tell you, when on speaking to him, he answered in a language of which I could not comprehend a word. We tried him in all sorts of ways, and he made a variety of signs, but we could not comprehend the meaning he intended to convey. In appearance he greatly resembled the slaves I had seen at Zanzibar, on board the Arab dhows, though better looking. Like most of them, he had but a clout round his waist, and his woolly hair was cropped close. Still he evidently did not lack intelligence. It was very tantalising to find that we could get no information out of him. The little girl was equally unable to give an account of herself, though I fancied that she understood us when we spoke English, but she could not reply intelligibly.

"I treated the black as he deserved, for the brave way in which he had saved the child, and he showed that he was grateful for such kindness as I bestowed upon him.

"As to the little girl, though I made inquiries at every place I touched at, I could get no information by which I could even guess where she had come from or who she was. From her ways and tone of voice I felt sure, however, that she was of gentle birth. The black seemed mortally afraid of the Arabs, and kept below when any came on board or any dhows hove in sight; indeed it was some time

before we could make him understand that he was
safe with us, and that no one would venture to take
him away by force.   He soon became a great favourite
with the men, who gave him the name of Tom, in
addition to the one by which he called himself, which
sounded like Baraka, and Tom Baraka he has been
ever since.   In a short time he picked up a few words
of English, with which he managed to make himself
understood ; but it was not until we were on the
voyage home that he was able to give me an idea
how he and the little girl came to be on the piece of
wreck from which we rescued him.   I would call him
in, and let him give his own history ; but I think I
can make you understand the account better if I give it
in ordinary English, for I took no little trouble during
several months to get the truth out of him, anxious as
he was to give the information I required.   His vocabu-
lary being somewhat limited, he accompanied his
words by signs, often of so curious a description that
it was with difficulty my officers and I could restrain
ourselves from bursting into fits of laughter, and yet
his account was sad enough.

"I placed before him the best map I possessed of
the part of Africa from which I calculated he came, and
explained to him the rivers and lakes marked upon it.
He shook his head, as if he could make nothing of it,
but at last fixed on a spot some way in the interior.

" ' There !' he said, making a wide circle with his
finger, ' There abouts was my home.   By the banks

of a river which fell into a lake my people and I were happy in our way, we cultivated our fields and tended our cattle, and had abundance of food without thinking of the future. We heard, it is true, that the cruel men who come across from the big sea had carried off not a few of the inhabitaxes of other districts; but it was a long, long distance away, and we hoped they would never come near us. We lived as our fathers had done. Occasionally we had to fight to punish our neighbours, who came upon our land and tried to carry off our cattle; and as I grew up and increased in strength I became a warrior, but I only wished to fight to protect my home and my fields from our enemies. When old enough I married a wife, who was as fond of me as woman could be. When kindly treated black women love their husbands, as do their white sisters. We had a little child, I was fond of him, oh! so fond. My delight when I came in from the fields was to carry him about in my arms, or to roll with him on the grass, letting him tumble over me and pull my hair and ears, and then he would smile down into my face and laugh merrily. I was a hunter also, and used fearlessly to attack huge elephants for the sake of their tusks, as well as for their flesh, especially for their big feet, which afford a dainty meal. Even one would be sufficient for the whole of our party. I had crossed the river, with several companions, armed with bows, arrows, and spears, intending to go some distance south, where many elephants, it was said, had been seen. A stranger brought the account. We had gone a day's journey, and were encamped at night, hoping to fall in with a herd of elephants the next day. We had eaten our evening meal, and were about to lie down to sleep, when we were startled by hearing a shower of bullets come whistling above our heads. We rose to fly, but knew not which way to go, for from either side strange cries assailed our ears, and before we could recover from our surprise a large party of men, with gleaming swords in their hands, rushed in upon us. Snatching up our spears we attempted to defend ourselves, but were quickly overpowered, two of my friends being killed and others badly wounded. We were at once bound with cords and thrown on the ground, while our captors were employed in preparing another way to secure us. They were fierce men in dark dresses, some wearing turbans on their heads, others red caps. I watched their proceedings, thinking that, perhaps, they were going to kill and eat us. They cut down some young trees, leaving a fork at one end, and fixing a thick branch at the other, so as to form another fork. When several logs had thus been prepared, they made us with kicks get up, and picking out the strongest men among us, placed one at one end of a log, and one at the other, securing them by the forks round our necks. As our arms were lashed behind our backs we could offer no resistance, but, pricked by the spears or sword points of our captors, were compelled to march forward in the direction they ordered us. Twenty or more of us were thus secured; the remainder were fastened together by a long rope, one behind the other at an interval of a few feet, with their arms lashed behind them, led by an Arab. With the heavy log round our necks we had no chance of escaping, nor indeed had the others, who would have been shot had they made the attempt. Two or three of the worst wounded sank down from loss of blood. The Arabs made them get up and proceed, but finding at last that the poor wretches could not keep up with the rest, took them out of the line, and putting pistols to their heads, shot them dead. We were joined as we proceeded towards the coast by other captives, taken much as we had been, and treated in the same cruel manner. Some, who had come from still further up the country than we had, and who had thus a longer march, told us that one-third of their number had died or been killed on the way, so that even those who were suffering severely from sickness endeavoured to struggle on as long as they had strength to move for fear of being murdered.

"'At night we were ordered to lie down before the fire, with a strong guard placed over us. We were generally amply fed, in order that our strength might be kept up. Although we passed through several thickly-populated districts, no one dared to help us for fear of the Arabs. At length we reached the bank of a river, near the sea-coast, where we found a large vessel ready to receive us. We were at once ordered to go on board, when we were placed on a bamboo deck, packed close to each other, with our chins resting on our knees. As soon as some fifty or more of us were stowed on the lower deck, another deck was placed over our heads, preventing us even from sitting upright. On this another layer of slaves was stowed in the same way that we were. A third deck was placed above them, which was also crowded with unfortunate captives. We could hear the voices of those above us, and frequently their cries, as the Arabs beat them in order to make them sit closer. A narrow passage was left down the centre of the deck, along which the Arabs could pass to bring us our food. We were thus kept a couple of days in the river, either waiting for a fair wind, or because our masters were afraid of being caught by some of the ships of the white men. Our condition was bad enough in smooth water, but we were to find it considerably worse when we got into the open sea. My only consolation was that my wife and little boy had escaped. I knew that they would be mourning for me, whom they were never to see again. I then wished that they were dead, that their grief might come to an end; and sometimes a terrible thought came to me that they too might some day be captured and carried off to the same horrible slavery which I was doomed, as I thought, to bear. There were not only men on board, but women and children, to be taken to a far distant country, of which we had never before heard. Where it was we could not tell, but we knew, by one telling the other, that it was inhabited by the same sort of people as the Arabs, and we supposed that they would beat and otherwise cruelly treat us if we did not obey them. The younger women and children were better cared for than we men were, and were well fed, to make them look plump and healthy. The vessel had one great nearly triangular sail, and the after part rose high out of the water, while the bows seemed as if they would dip under it. At last, the wind being fair, we sailed. For some time we glided on. A few of us were sent on deck at a time to breath the fresh air. I felt my heart sink within me, when, on looking round, I could nowhere see the land, nothing but the smooth, shining ocean on every side. It was terrible; I thought we should never again set foot on shore. I had often paddled my canoe on the river, and had even made trading voyages down to the great lake, where I had seen huge waves covered with foam rolling across it; but on such occasions we had quickly made for the shore. Twice my canoe had been upset, but I had easily gained it by swimming. Suddenly the wind began to roar, the thunder rolled above our heads, and the dhow was tossed about by the sea in a way which made me expect that she would speedily be

thrown over, and that all on board would be sent into
the raging waves. Pitiful were the shrieks and cries
of my companions. In vain the Arabs ordered them
to keep quiet; they believed that their last hour was
come, and cared not what was said to them. I determined, whatever happened, to struggle for my life. I
was young and strong; and the thought entered my
mind that I might swim to the shore, and get back
some day to my wife and children, though I knew
that my home must be a long way off. I felt quite
disappointed when the storm ceased, and the dhow
glided on her course as before. When I next went
on deck, I saw that she was in company with other
vessels, rigged as she was, and sailing in the same
direction. Each of them had prisoners on board.
The decks of two or three of the larger ones were
crowded with black forms, and I guessed that there
were as many more below. Our dhow sailed very
fast, and was passing most of them, when a calm
came on, and we lay all huddled together, near enough
for the people in one vessel to speak to those on board
another. Presently I heard the Arabs shouting to
each other that there was a large sail in sight. The
news seemed to alarm them. She was coming towards the fleet of dhows, bringing up a breeze. At
last the wind filled our sails, and the dhows began to
separate. We fancied that if we could keep ahead of
the stranger that she could not harm us; but we saw
flashes of flame proceeding from her side, and round

shot came bounding over the water towards us; first one dhow was hit, now another. At last one shot struck our vessel, going through the side, and fearful were the cries which arose from the people below, who were wounded, or expected to be killed by other shots. I had been allowed to remain on deck, for the Arabs in their flight did not think about the slaves. I saw some of the dhows lower their sails, when boats from the big ship took possession of them. Our dhow sailing faster than the others soon got ahead, and I saw our Arab masters rejoicing that they should escape; but the wind was increasing; every instant it grew stronger and stronger. The large sail was lowered, and a small one hoisted, but we dashed over the fast rising sea at greater speed than ever, soon losing sight of the big ship, which, after securing the prizes she had taken, pursued some other dhows, who were endeavouring to make their escape in different directions to that we were steering. The storm, however, increased. The Arabs now began to look alarmed. In vain they tried to stop the hole which the shot had made in the vessel's side; finding this difficult, owing to the crowd of slaves below, they began to throw those in their way overboard. Some were dead, others wounded, but many were uninjured. They shrieked out for mercy, but the Arabs heeded them not.

" 'I had kept in the fore part of the vessel, hidden behind a coil of rope, fully expecting that they would soon seize me. After labouring away for some time and finding the water come in as fast as ever, they began to lower a boat and canoe, for the purpose of getting into them, and trying to save their lives, intending to leave me and my companions to our fate. The sea was foaming and roaring around us. It seemed that at any moment the dhow would sink. The sail was now lowered, and the boat and canoe were got into the water. The cry arose that the dhow was sinking, and the Arabs leapt into them in such haste that the boat was upset, and all in her were speedily overwhelmed. The canoe, after being tossed about on the tops of the waves for a few minutes, was also turned over, and all in her shared the fate of their companions. She was not far off at the time. I thought that I might reach her, but I remembered my fellow-slaves. I found a knife which one of the Arabs had left on the deck, and was endeavouring to release some of the men, who might be able to swim with me to the canoe, when I felt that the dhow was going down. I sprang overboard, and with a few strokes gained the canoe, being almost thrown on to her by the seas, when I felt that she was being drawn under the surface; but I clutched tight hold of her, and she quickly came up again. For a few moments the shrieks and cries of my drowning countrymen rose high above the loud dashing of the waves and the howling of the storm, but they were speedily silenced, and I found myself floating alone on the tossing waters. I wished to live for the sake of my

wife and child. In my ignorance I knew not how far
I was away from the land, still I struggled for life.
All night long I clung to the canoe, and before
morning the wind had fallen and the sea had become
smooth. I was able to right the canoe, when I saw
close to me a gourd and a paddle. I reached them by
working the canoe on with my hands, and contrived to
bale her out. I saw the sun rise, and knew that the
land lay on the opposite side. I tried to paddle towards
it; but I had had no food and no water, and the sun came
down with a heat I had never felt on shore. Still, for
hours I paddled on, when I saw the sails of a big ship
rising above the horizon. She must be, I thought, the
one which had captured the dhows. Fear filled my
heart, for the Arabs had told us that the white men
would kill and eat us. Terror and the suffering I had
undergone overcame me; I sank down at the bottom
of the canoe, and knew no more until I found myself
on board a ship, with white people standing round me.
I could not understand a word they said, nor tell
them how I came to be in the canoe, but they looked
kind, and my fears left me. I was well fed and cared
for, and soon recovered my strength. There were
several persons whom I now know to have been passengers. One lady, very fair and beautiful, who spoke in
a gentle, sweet voice to me, trying to make me comprehend what she meant. She had a little girl with her.
I loved that child from the first, for she made me think
of my own boy by her playful ways and happy laugh,

though she was fair as a lily, and my boy was as black
as I am, but I thought not of the difference of colour.
I felt that I should never wish to leave that kind lady
and her child. In a few days the weather again
became bad, a fearful gale began to blow. The ship
was tossed about far more violently than the dhow had
been. Presently, during the night, I heard a loud
crash, followed by the shouts and shrieks of the crew
and passengers. My first thought was of the little
girl. On reaching the deck a flash of lightning showed
her to me, clinging to her mother's arms. I made
signs that I would try and save her, and I wrapped her
up in some shawls which had been brought from below.
The officers and crew were, I saw, trying to lower the
boats. Whether they succeeded or not I could not
tell, for the seas were sweeping over the ship, and I
knew too that she was sinking, as the dhow had done.
While I was standing by the lady's side, looking for
one of the boats into which to help her, a huge sea
separated us, carrying me off my legs, and I found
myself struggling amid the foaming waves. I had
caught sight of a dark object floating near, far larger
than a boat. By what means I know not I reached
it. It was part of the wreck of a dhow or of some other
vessel against which our ship had struck. I climbed
upon it with my little charge, whose head I had
managed to keep above water. She was crying out for
her mamma. I knew that name. I tried to console her.
For some time voices reached my ear, but whether

they came from the boats or the deck of the ship I could not tell; I guessed, too truly, that she had gone down, for when morning at last dawned neither she nor the boats were to be seen. I feared that the little girl would sink from hunger and thirst, for I remembered what I had endured in the canoe; but scarcely had the sun risen than I saw a ship approaching, and you, Massa Pack, know the rest.'

"It was my ship which Tom saw coming. Of course we soon had him and his little charge on board. You will understand that I have given what I may call a translation of his yarn. It was spun, as it were, in a number of shreds, and I have put them together; still I have expressed his sentiments, and have not adorned his tale by adding to it anything he did not say. Many a time did he melt into tears as he spoke of his own child and the love he bore him, and it would be difficult to picture fully all the horrors he endured during his journey overland and his voyage in the slave dhow. To send him back to his home I knew was impossible, he would have been retaken by the first Arab party he fell in with, or been murdered as he was trying to pass through the territory of any hostile tribe. He therefore cheerfully remained on board my ship, and has stayed with me ever since, pretty well reconciled to his lot, his whole soul wrapped up in Mary, who has taken the place in his affections of the son from whom he has, he believes, for ever been separated, though he is devoted also to

my sister, and to Ned and me. That black fellow
has as big a heart as any white man. He does not,
however, forget his wife and child, for since he became
a Christian, his great desire is that they should be
brought to a knowledge of the truth. If it were
possible, I would help him to get back to his native
village, but to do so is beyond my means. Indeed,
from what I hear I fear that the Arabs have long ere
this carried them off into captivity, or that, deprived
of their protector, they have died of hunger or been
killed by their cruel persecutors. Those Arabs have
long been the curse of that part of Africa—indeed, for
the purpose of obtaining slaves, they have devastated
many of its most fertile districts."

His guest listened with evident interest to the
account given by the lieutenant.

"I have not hitherto turned my attention in that
direction," observed the former. "Of course I have
heard much of the slave trade on the western coast
and of the horrors of the middle passage, but I
believed that it is now carried on only in a very
limited degree, and that the inhabitants of the east
coast are well able to take care of themselves."

"I have cruised on both coasts, and am convinced
that the people on the east part of Africa are subjected to cruelties fully equal to those which the
western tribes have for so many ages endured,"
answered the lieutenant. "Tom's experience is
that of thousands; but he did not describe the

miseries suffered by those left behind, the despair of
the women and children, and of the men who may
have escaped from the sudden attack made on their
village, to find it when they have returned burned to
the ground, their fields laid waste, and their cattle
carried off. No one can calculate the numbers who
have died from hunger in a land teeming with
abundance."

Ned and Mary came in during the latter part of
the conversation, to which they paid the greatest
attention.

"I wish I could help to put a stop to such horrible
doings," exclaimed Ned. "I should like to see an
English fleet employed in catching all the dhows, and
an army sent to march through the country to turn
all the Arabs out of it. It would be an honour to
serve even as a drummer-boy on shore, or as a
powder-monkey on board one of the ships."

Their guest smiled at Ned's enthusiasm.

"A more certain way may be found for benefiting
the Africans than by armies or fleets," observed Miss
Sarah; "if a band of faithful missionaries of the
Gospel were scattered through the country, they
would, with God's blessing, carry Christianity and
civilisation to the long benighted and cruelly treated
people."

"You speak the truth, madam, the matter is
worthy of consideration," observed the guest, turning
to Miss Sarah. "I have learned several things since

I came into your house.   I wish that I could remain
longer to learn more, but I am compelled to go up to
London; and as I feel myself sufficiently strong to
travel, I must, early to-morrow morning, wish you
farewell."

CHAPTER III.

THE shipwrecked stranger had taken his departure; he had paid the doctor, and sent a present to the coast-guard men who had assisted to carry him to the house; but he had not offered to remunerate the lieutenant or Tom for the service they had rendered him, though he feelingly expressed his gratitude to them. Perhaps he considered, and he was not wrong in so doing, that they not only did not require a reward for performing an act of humanity, but would have felt hurt had it been offered them.

The next morning the lieutenant and Ned started on a walk along the cliffs to inquire at Longview station about the coast-guard man who had nearly been killed on the night of the wreck. The sky was clear, the blue ocean slumbered below their feet, the gentle ripples which played over it sparkling in the bright rays of the sun. A large vessel, with a wide spread of canvas, was gliding majestically by on her way down channel. Ned gazed at her with a wistful eye.

"I wish that I were on board that fine craft," he said at length. "I am very happy at home, and I don't want to leave you and Aunt Sally and Mary, but I feel that I ought to be doing something for myself. You and my father went to sea before you were as old as I am. I don't like to be idle and a burden to you. If you did not disapprove of it, I would go before the mast and work my way up— many have done so who are now masters in the merchant service; though, as you know, I would rather go into the navy, but from what you tell me that is out of the question. The owners of your old ship would, I dare say, take me as an apprentice; I'll try and do my duty, and learn to be a sailor so as to become an officer as soon as possible."

"You look far ahead; but it is all right, my boy, and I am very sure of one thing, that you will do your duty and reap the reward, whatever happens. I'll write to Clew, Earring, & Grummet, and ask them if they have a vacancy for you. Jack Clew, who was once in the navy, was a messmate of mine on board the old 'Thunderer' when I lost my leg at 'Navarin'" (so the lieutenant always pronounced Navarino, the action fought by the British fleet under Sir Edward Codrington with that of the Turks and Egyptians). "Jack used to profess a willingness to serve me, but, Ned, we must not trust too much to old friends. Times alter, and he may find he has applicants nearer at hand whose relatives have longer purses than I have. Don't fear, however, my boy, something may turn up, as it always does, if we seek diligently to get it and wait with patience."

Ned did not then press the matter further; his spirits were buoyant, and although his uncle's remarks were not calculated to raise them, he was not disheartened.

Edward Garth, the lieutenant's nephew, was the son of a younger sister, who had married a friend and messmate, a lieutenant in the same noble service in which he had spent his best days. They had served together in several ships up to the time that Garth was stricken down with fever up an African river, their ship then forming one of the blockading squadron on the west coast, when he committed his infant boy to his brother-in-law's care. "I am sure that you will look after him for our poor Fanny's sake; but she is delicate, and I know not what effect my death will have on her. At all events, he will be fatherless, and she, poor girl, will find it a hard matter to manage a spirited lad."

"Do not let that thought trouble you, Ned," answered Lieutenant Pack; "Fanny's child shall ever be as if he were my own son. I promised to keep house with Sally, and Fanny shall come and live with us. A better soul than Sally does not exist, though I, who am her brother, say so."

Soon after he had seen his brother-in-law laid in the grave, Lieutenant Pack came home to find that his sister Fanny had followed her husband to the other world, and that Sally had already taken charge of their young nephew.

From that day forward she truly became a mother to the orphan, and as the lieutenant proved a kind, though not over indulgent father, Ned never felt the loss of his parents, and grew up all that his uncle and aunt could desire, rewarding them for their watchful care and judicious management of him. The lieutenant's means would not allow him to bestow an expensive education on his nephew, but he was enabled to send him to a neighbouring grammar school, where the boy, diligently taking advantage of such instruction as it afforded, soon reached the head of each class in which he was placed. Though first in all manly exercises, he made good use of his books at home, his uncle giving him lessons in mathematics and navigation, so that he was as well prepared for the profession he desired to enter as any boy of his age. Ned was a favourite with all who knew him. His home training had answered, for, though kind, it had been judicious. He was truthful and honest, and sincerely-desirous of doing his duty, while he was manly and good-tempered, ever ready to forgive an injury, though well capable of standing up for himself. Had the " Worcester " training-ship then been estab-lished, and had Ned gone on board her, he would probably have become a gold medallist, and that is saying much in his favour. His uncle delighted in his society—"Ned always made him feel young again," he used to say—and Aunt Sally bestowed upon him the affection of her kind and gentle heart. As to Mary, she thought there never had been, never could be, a boy equal to brother Ned, for so she always called him, ever looking on him as her brother. Ned faithfully returned the affectionate feelings evinced towards him by his relatives.

The one-legged lieutenant and his nephew continued their walk, the former stopping every now and then to impress a remark on Ned, or glancing over the ocean to observe the progress made by the outward-bound ship, until the row of whitewashed cottages, surmounted by a signal staff, which formed the coast-guard station of Longview, hove in sight. Lieutenant Hanson, who met them at a short distance from it, shook Ned and his uncle cordially by the hand.

"We came to learn how poor Herron is getting on," said the lieutenant.

"He'll weather it, I hope; but it was a wonder he was not killed from his fall down the cliff, sixty feet, with exposure to the rain and wind during the whole of the night, for we did not find him until the morning," answered the coast-guard officer. "The accident was even of more consequence to others than to himself, for had it not occurred, we might have been in time to save some more of the poor fellows from the wreck."

"That may be so; but had you come, my black man Tom Baraka and Ned here would have lost the opportunity of showing what they are made of, by pulling one of them out of the water," said Lieutenant Pack.

"What! had you a hand in saving the passenger?" asked Lieutenant Hanson, turning to Ned.

"Indeed he had, and had it not been for his courage I believe that the man would have been washed away again, for Tom was pretty well exhausted by that time," answered Lieutenant Pack.

"You have begun well," said Mr. Hanson, casting an approving look at Ned.

"He has set his heart on going to sea, though I fear there is but little chance of his getting into the navy," observed Lieutenant Pack.

"If he does, I hope that he may be more fortunate than some of his elders," answered the coast-guard lieutenant in a tone not very encouraging.

The remark produced a momentary effect on Ned, but he soon forgot it, and was as eager as before to become a sailor.

They proceeded on to the station, where, after visiting the injured man, for whom the old lieutenant had brought some delicacies made by Miss Sarah, he and his nephew set off to return home by a circuitous road, which ran a good way inland. They had got some way, when they caught sight of Miss Sarah and Mary in the distance.

"Go, Ned, and see where those women-kind of ours are bound for," exclaimed the lieutenant.

Ned ran forward.

"We are going to visit Silas Shank the miser, as the people call him, though he must be very poor and miserable, as I cannot suppose that he would nearly starve himself if he had the means of buying proper food," answered Mary.

"If I may, I will go with you," said Ned; "perhaps Uncle Pack would like to come also."

The lieutenant, for whom they waited, however, preferred going home, and Miss Sally, giving her basket to Ned, returned with him, allowing her nephew to accompany Mary.

"Just leave the pudding and jelly with the old man, and if he does not appear inclined to talk do not stop," said Miss Sally.

Ned and Mary walked on, cheerfully conversing, as they were wont to do, for they had always plenty to say to each other, and Mary's tongue wagged as fast as that of any young lady of her age, though not so thoughtlessly as that of many. Ned naturally spoke of the ship he had seen running down channel. "I do not wish to be away from you all, but yet I did wish to be on board her, sailing to distant lands, to go among strange people, and to feel that I was doing something and learning to be an officer. It would be a fine thing to command a ship like that."

"I wish as you wish; but, O Ned, you would be a long, long time absent from us—months and months, or perhaps years and years. Uncle Pack says that he was once five years without setting foot on English ground, and you might be as long away. We shouldn't know you when you came back; you will be grown into a big man, with a bronzed face and bushy whiskers." Mary laughed, though the tears at the same time came into her eyes.

"But that was in the war-time, Mary, and even the Queen's ships are not now kept out for so long a period, while merchant vessels return every year, and sometimes from short voyages much oftener. And then think of all the curiosities I should bring home; I should delight in collecting them for you and Aunt Sally, or to add to Uncle Pack's museum."

"Yes, yes, it would be a very joyous time when you did come back, we should be delighted to see all the things you brought; but then think how slowly the days will pass by when you are away, uncle and aunt and I all alone."

"There would be only one less," said Ned, naturally.

"Yes, I know," answered Mary—she stopped short—she did not say how large a space Ned occupied in her world. She was not aware of it herself just then.

The subject was one which made her feel sadder than was her wont, and she was glad to change it.

Old Shank's cottage was soon reached. It stood about half a mile from the village. It was situated in a hollow, an old quarry, by the side of a hill, the bare downs rising beyond it without a tree near. A desolate-looking place in its best days. Though containing several rooms—a large part of the roof having fallen in—it had only one which was habitable. In that lived Silas Shank the reputed miser. The palings which fenced it in had been broken down to be used as firewood. The gate was off its hinges ; nettles and other hardy weeds had taken possession of the garden. Scarcely a pane of glass remained in any of the windows ; even those of the rooms occupied by the miser were stuffed with rags, or had pieces of brown paper pasted over them.

"I'll stay outside while you go in," said Ned ; "the old man was very surly when I last saw him, and I do not wish to face him again. He can't be rough to you."

Mary knocked at the door, which was tightly closed.

" Who's there ? " asked a tremulous voice.

"It is I, Mary Pack ; I've brought you something from aunt which she thought you would like to have."

The bars were withdrawn.

" Come in ! " said the same voice, and the door was cautiously opened.

Mary, without hesitation, entered in time to see a

thin old man, in a tattered threadbare great-coat, with
a red woollen cap on his head, and slippered feet, his
stockings hanging about his ancles, totter back to an
arm-chair from which he had risen, by the side of a
small wood fire on which a pot was boiling.

"That's all I've got for my dinner, with a few
potatoes, but it's enough to keep body and soul
together, and what more does a wretched being like
me want?" he said in a querulous voice.

"I have brought you something nice, as aunt knows
you can't cook anything of the sort yourself, and you
may eat it with more appetite than you can the
potatoes," said Mary, placing the contents of the
basket in some cracked plates on a rickety three-legged
table which stood near the old man's chair.

He eagerly eyed the tempting-looking pudding, a
nicely cooked chop, and a delicious jelly. "Yes, that's
more like what I once used to have," he muttered.
"Thank you, thank you, little girl. I cannot buy such
things for myself, but I am glad to get them from
others. Sit down, pray do, after your walk," and he
pointed to a high-backed oak chair, of very doubtful
stability and covered with dust. He saw that Mary
on that account hesitated to sit down, so rising he
shambled forward and wiped it with an old cotton
handkerchief which he drew out of his pocket. "There,
now it's all clean and nice; you must sit down and rest,
and see me eat the food, so that you may tell your aunt
I sold none of it The people say that I have parted

with my coat off my back and the shoes from my feet, but do not believe them; if I did, it was on account of my poverty."

Mary made no reply; it appeared to her that the old man was contradicting himself, and she did not wish to inquire too minutely into the matter.

"This pudding must have cost a great deal," he continued, as he ate it mouthful by mouthful; "there's the flour, the milk, the raisins, and the sugar and spice, and other ingredients. Your aunt must be a rich woman to afford so dainty a dish for a poor man like me?"

"No, I do not think Aunt Sally is at all rich, but she saves what little she can to give to the sick and needy; she heard that you were ill, Mr. Shank, and had no one to care for you."

"That's true, little girl, no one cares for the old miser, as they call me; and the boys, when I go into the village, throw stones at me, and jeer and shout at my heels. I hate boys!"

'I'm sure Ned would not do that," said Mary; "he is always kind and gentle, and would beat off bad boys if he saw them treating you in that way."

"No, he wouldn't, he would join them, and behave like the rest. They are all alike, boys! Mischievous little imps!"

Mary felt very indignant at hearing Ned thus designated, but she repressed her rising anger, pitying the forlorn old man, and smiling, said,

"You will find you are mistaken in regard to Ned, Mr. Shank; he is outside, and I must not keep him waiting longer. But I was nearly forgetting that I have a book to give you, which Aunt Sally thought you would like to read. It is in large print, so that you need not try your eyes."

Mary, as she spoke, produced a thin book from her basket, and presented it to the old man. He glanced at it with indifference.

"I do not care about this sort of thing," he said. "I wonder people spend money in having such productions printed. A loss of time to print them, and a loss of time to read them!"

"Aunt Sally will be much disappointed if you do not keep the book," said Mary, quietly; "you might like to read it when you are all alone and have nothing else to do."

"Well, well, as she has sent me the pudding, I'll keep the book; she means kindly, I dare say, and I do not wish to make you carry it back. What! must you go, little girl? You'll come and see me again some day, and bring another nice pudding, won't you?" said the old man, looking at Mary with a more amiable expression in his eyes than they generally wore.

"Yes, I must go, I cannot, indeed, keep Ned waiting longer. Good-bye, Mr. Shank; you'll read the book, and I'll tell Aunt Sally what you say," said Mary, taking up her basket and tripping out of the room.

" Don't let that boy Ned you spoke of throw stones in at my window. You see how others have broken the panes, and it would cost too much money to have them repaired."

He said this as he followed Mary with a shuffling step to the door.

" Ned would never dream of doing anything of the sort," she answered, now feeling greatly hurt at the remark.

" They 're all alike, they 're all alike," muttered the old man ; " but you, I dare say, can keep him in order. I didn't mean to offend you, little girl," he added, observing Mary's grave look, as she turned round to wish him good-bye before going through the doorway.

The remark pacified her. " Poor old man !" she thought, " sickness makes him testy."

" Good-bye, little girl," said Mr. Shank, as he stood with his hand on the door-latch ; " you 'll come again soon ? "

" If Aunt Sally sends me ; but you must promise not to accuse Ned wrongfully. Good-bye !" answered Mary, as she stepped over the threshold, the old man immediately closing and bolting the door.

Ned, who had been on the watch at a little distance, sprang forward to meet her. She did not tell him what old Mr. Shank had said, as she naturally thought that it would make him indignant ; and like a wise girl she confined herself merely to saying how glad he seemed to be to get the food, and how poor and wretched he looked.

Mary and Ned had a pleasant walk home. After this she paid several visits to old Mr. Shank, sometimes with Aunt Sally, at others with the lieutenant and Ned, but she always carried the basket and presented the contents to the old man. Aunt Sally would not believe that he was really a miser, although the people called him one. The cottage was his own, and he obtained periodically a few shillings at the bank, but this was all he was known to possess, and the amount was insufficient to supply him with the bare necessaries of life. He picked up sticks and bits of coal which fell from carts for firing. He possessed a few goats, which lived at free quarters on the downs, and their winter food cost but little. He sold the kids and part of the milk which he did not consume. He seemed grateful to Mary, and talked to her more than to any one else ; but to Aunt Sally and the lieutenant he rarely uttered a word beyond a cold expression of thanks for the gifts they bestowed upon him.

Ned in the meantime was waiting anxiously for an answer to the letter his uncle had written Messrs. Clew, Earring, & Grummet, the shipowners. After some delay a reply was received from a clerk, stating that Mr. Clew was dead, and that the other partners were unable to comply with the lieutenant's request unless a considerable premium was paid, which was utterly beyond his means.

This was a great disappointment to Ned.

"Don't fret over it, my boy," said his uncle, "we shall all find many things to bear up against through life. There's a good time coming for all of us, if we'll only wait patiently for it. I ought to have been an admiral, and so I might if my leg hadn't been knocked away by a Turkish round shot at Navarin; but you see, notwithstanding, I am as happy as a prince. As far as I myself am concerned I have no reasonable want unsupplied, though I should like to have your very natural wish complied with."

Still week after week went by; the lieutenant wrote several other letters, but the answers were unsatisfactory. At last he began to talk of going up himself to town to call on the Admiralty, and to beard the lions in their den; but it was an undertaking the thoughts of which he dreaded far more than had he been ordered to head a boarding party against an enemy's ship. He talked the matter over with his sister Sally.

"If we want a thing we must go for it, if we don't want it we may stay at home and not get it," he observed. "If I felt anything like sure that I should succeed by pressing my claim, I'd go ten times as far; but my belief is, that I shall be sent back with a flea in my ear."

"Still, what can poor Ned do if he doesn't go to sea, though I wish that we could have found him some employment on shore suited to his taste," said Miss Sarah.

"Well, I'll make up my mind about the matter," said the lieutenant, who was as anxious as his sister to forward Ned's wishes. "I can but ask, you know, and if I am refused, I shall have good reason for grumbling for the next year to come, or to the end of my days. I'll go and talk the subject over with Hanson; he knows more about the ways of the Admiralty than I do, and will give me a wrinkle or two. In the meantime do you get my old uniform brushed up and my traps ready."

Next morning the old lieutenant, summoning Ned, set off to pay a visit to his brother officer. Ned was in high spirits at hearing that steps were actually being taken to promote his object, and he expressed his gratitude to his uncle for the effort he was about to make on his behalf. All diffi-culties seemed to vanish, and he already saw himself a midshipman on board a fine ship sailing down channel.

Lieutenant Hanson was not very sanguine when he heard of his friend's intention.

"There is nothing like asking, however, and they can't eat you, though you may be refused," he answered. "Go by all means; get to the Admiralty early, step boldly in, and show that you fully expect to have your request granted. Say that the boy will soon be over age, and consequently there is no time to be lost."*

Although the old lieutenant had not received much encouragement from Mr. Hanson, yet some of the difficulties he had apprehended appeared to clear away, and he walked home with Ned, resolved to carry out his project. The cost of his expedition was now his chief anxiety. He pictured to himself the risk of running short of funds in the great metropolis, and being unable to pay his journey back. Then Sally would be hard put to it for many a long month.

"His small income, poor lad, won't go far to defray his outfit and allowance," he said to himself as he walked along. "Still it must be done, and we'll find the ways and means. If the worst comes to the worst, I'll go to sea, and take Ned with me. I wonder I never thought of that before. It will make some amends to him for not entering the navy; he'd soon become a prime seaman under my charge, and in a few years get the command of a ship."

Such were some of the thoughts which passed through the worthy officer's mind, but he did not express them aloud.

While pointing his telescope seaward, an employ-

---

* At the period we are speaking of, the rule had not been formed which makes it necessary for boys to undergo a training on board the "Britannia" before they can become midshipmen. The Admiralty either appointed them to ships, or captains had the privilege of taking a certain number selected by themselves.

ment in which he seldom failed to spend a part of the day, he caught sight of a cutter standing for the bay.

As the tide had just turned, and the wind was falling, it was evident that she was about to bring up. In a short time her commander, Lieutenant Jenkins, came on shore, and proved to be an old messmate of Mr. Pack. On hearing of his intention of going to London, Lieutenant Jenkins at once offered him a passage as far as Portsmouth. The invitation was gladly accepted, as a considerable expense would thus be saved. Miss Sally having packed her brother's traps, he, late in the evening, went on board the cutter, which, just as darkness set in, sailed for the westward.

CHAPTER IV.

SEVERAL days had passed by, and no news had been received from the lieutenant. Aunt Sally began to grow anxious, though she pursued her ordinary avocations in her usual calm manner. Desirous as she was of being economical, she did not forget poor old Mr. Shank, and Mary and Ned were despatched with some provisions which she had prepared, and another book from her lending-library for him. Mary, remembering his dislike to boys, went in alone, leaving Ned to amuse himself outside.

"I'll not be long, and I want you to walk up and down out of sight of his window, or he may, if he sees you, say something unpleasant," observed Mary.

Ned, though he cared very little as to what the old man might say about him, did not wish to have Mary's feelings hurt, and promising obedience, walked on to a spot whence he could watch for her when she came out.

She rapped at the door, the bolts were withdrawn, and she entered.

"Glad to see you, little girl," said Mr. Shank, as he led the way into his room. "No one has come here for many a day. I am well-nigh starving, for the people in the village yonder do not trouble themselves about the wretched old miser, as they call me; and I could not go out yesterday to buy food—if I did, where was I to get the money to pay for it?"

"Aunt, fearing that you might be in want, has sent you something to eat," said Mary, unpacking her basket, and placing the contents on the three-legged table.

The old man drew it towards him, and began to eat far more voraciously than usual, showing that in one respect at all events his assertion was correct. Mary, thinking that it might amuse him, mentioned the lieutenant's journey to London and its object.

"So they intend to send that boy off to sea! The best thing they can do with him. Boys are always up to mischief at home, and it is to be hoped he'll never come back."

"You should not say that, Mr. Shank!" exclaimed Mary, indignantly. "Ned is a good honest boy, he never harmed you in any way, and if he had it is your duty to forgive him, for God tells us in His Word to forgive our enemies, and do good to those who ill-treat us."

"I don't understand that; if we are not to hate our enemies, who and what are we to hate?" muttered the old man.

"We are to hate nothing except sin and Satan, because that is what God hates, I am very sure," said Mary. "Doesn't the book I brought you last week say that? And here is another which aunt has sent you, perhaps you will like to read it," and she put the volume on the table.

"What the book says doesn't concern me. I do no harm to any one; all I want is to lead a quiet life and be let alone," he muttered, evidently not wishing to enter into a discussion with the little girl, fearing perhaps that he might lose his temper. He, however, took the book she had brought and gave her back the other, observing, "Perhaps your aunt will lend it me at some other time if I feel ill and fancy I am going to die; but I shan't die yet, O no, no, I want to live a great many years longer."

"I hope that you may, if you wish it," said Mary. She did not add, "I wonder what the poor old man can find so pleasant in his existence as to make him desire to live?" She did not again refer to Ned, but shortly got up, and told Mr. Shank that she must be going.

"What! do you come all this way alone merely to visit a wretched being like me?" he exclaimed, as she moved towards the door.

"No, Ned comes with me, and he is waiting to take me back," she answered.

"Why didn't he come in and sit down until you were ready to go?" he asked.

"Because, Mr. Shank, he knows that you dislike boys," said Mary.

"Perhaps, as you think so well of him, he may not be so bad as others. When you come again bring him in; I'll not scold him if he speaks civilly to me, and doesn't attempt to play me tricks."

"He'll not play you tricks, and I'm sure that he'll speak properly to you," answered Mary, considerably mollified by Mr. Shank's last remark. She was glad, however, that Ned was not in sight, as she still somewhat mistrusted the old man. As soon as the door was closed she looked about for Ned, and spied him hurrying up.

"He wants to see you," she said when Ned joined her, "so you must come in when Aunt Sally next sends me to him. He is a strange being. I wonder how he can manage to spend his time all by himself?"

They walked home chattering merrily, though Ned was a little more thoughtful than usual, wondering why his uncle had not written; and as soon as he had seen Mary safe at home, he hurried off to consult Lieutenant Hanson about the matter.

"Why," said Ned to the lieutenant, "has uncle not written?"

"Simply that he has had nothing to say, or has had no time to write, or if he has written, his letter may have gone astray," answered the lieutenant. "You must exercise patience, my young friend ; you 'll find plenty of that required in this world."

Ned returned home not much wiser than he went, but a brisk walk and the fresh air revived his spirits.

Next morning's post brought the looked-for letter, addressed to Miss Sarah Pack. She hurriedly opened it, while the young people looked eagerly on, watching her countenance. That, however, betrayed no satisfaction. The lieutenant's handwriting required time to decipher, though the characters were bold enough and covered a large sheet of paper.

"Dear Sally," it began, "I have been to the Admiralty and seen the First Lord, having reached this big city, and lost my way half-a-dozen times in it, four days after I left you. We had calms and light winds the whole distance to Portsmouth. His lordship received me with a profound bow, as if I had been an admiral, listened attentively to all I had to say, and I made up my mind that he was the politest gentleman I had ever met, and fully intended to grant my request. When I had finished, he glanced his eye down a long list, which he held up so that I could see it, remarking that there were a number of promising lads who desired to enter the service, but that he much feared he should be compelled to disappoint them. My claims were great, and he was surprised that his predecessors had not acknowledged them by promoting me ; that he had no doubt my brother-in-law would have been

an ornament to the service had he lived; that I
ought to have sent his son's name in long ago, and
that he would take the matter into consideration.
He desired me to leave my address, advising me not
to remain in town, as it might be some time before
I was likely to hear from him; he then politely
bowed me out of the room.   Whether or not anything will come of it is more than I can divine. In my
humble opinion my visit to London will prove bootless;
it can't be helped, Sally, so cheer up, and don't let Ned
get out of spirits.   I am going to call on two or three
shipowners, of whom Jenkins, who knows more of
London than I do, has told me, for if Ned cannot get
into the navy, he must make up his mind to enter the
merchant service.   I'll write more when I have more
to communicate, so, with love to the young ones, I
remain, your affectionate brother, John Pack."

Aunt Sally had to confess to herself that the
letter was not encouraging, still she did her best to
follow her brother's advice.   "Perhaps the First
Lord doesn't like to make promises, but he must be
a good man, or he would not hold the position he
does, and I dare say he'll do his best.   We may
have a letter even before your uncle comes back,
saying that you are appointed to a ship.   It can't be
so difficult a thing to make a midshipman.   Had
your uncle, however, asked to be promoted, I should
not have been surprised had he been refused.   It is
very kind of the First Lord to receive him so well and

to listen to all he had to say; we should not expect too much from great men."

Miss Sally ran on in the same strain for some time, but all she said failed to impart much confidence to poor Ned; still his uncle might succeed in getting him on board a merchant vessel, and like a prudent lad, he was ready for whatever might turn up. Next morning Ned eagerly looked out for the postman, but no letter arrived; another and another day passed by. It was too evident that the lieutenant had no news to communicate.

Some days after, just as evening was approaching, a post chaise was seen slowly descending the winding road which led down to the cottage. Miss Sally, followed by Ned, Mary, and Tom, hurried out. Ned darted forward to let down the steps, while Tom opened the door. The lieutenant, leaning on the black's shoulder, stepped out. Though he smiled at seeing those he loved, his countenance showed that he had no good news to communicate.

" I 'll tell you all about it when I have refreshed the inner man," he said, as, after paying the driver and telling Tom to look after him, he stumped into the house; "I am at present somewhat sharp set. It is several hours since I took anything on board in the shape of provisions, and my jaw tackles want greasing before I can make them work."

Aunt Sally and Mary quickly got supper ready, and the lieutenant having said grace, took his seat at the table. Having eaten a few mouthfuls he looked more cheerful than he had hitherto done. His sister and the young people were longing to hear what he had got to say.

"I told you I did not expect much from my visit to London, but it is wrong to allow ourselves to be cast down because things don't go as smoothly as we could wish," he at length observed. "I wrote you about my visit to the Admiralty; well, after that, believing that their lordships were not likely to do much for me, I called on three shipowners to whom Jenkins had given me introductions. They were civil enough, but all gave me the same sort of answer. They had numerous applications to receive on board their ships youngsters whose friends could pay handsome premiums, and in duty to themselves they were compelled to accept such in preference to others, willing as they were to attend to the recommendation of Lieutenant Jenkins. When I offered to take command of one of their ships, they replied, that as I had been some time on shore I might have grown rusty, and that they were obliged to employ officers brought up in their own service, though they could not doubt my abilities, and were duly grate ful for the offer I had made them. They would consider the matter, and let me know the result to which they might come, but no promise could be made on the subject."

Miss Sally looked greatly relieved when she heard that it was not likely her brother would go to sea, anxious as she was that poor Ned should obtain the object of his wishes.

"We must not despair, however," said the lieutenant. "We know that God orders all for the best, if we trust Him and do our duty; perhaps something will turn up when we least expect it. I have been thinking, Ned, how I can raise money enough to pay the required premium, and if I can do that the matter will be quickly settled. After two or three voyages to India, Australia, or round Cape Horn, you will have obtained sufficient experience to become a mate. You will then be independent and able to gain your own livelihood."

"That is what I wish to do, uncle," answered Ned, gulping down his disappointment at the thoughts that he should be unable to enter the navy, and some day become a Nelson or a Collingwood. In truth, matters stood very much as they were before the lieutenant's journey, and he had to confess to himself that the cost and trouble had apparently been thrown away.

"Well, well, Ned, we 'll go on with our mathematics and navigation, and wait patiently for what may occur. You are young yet, and won't be the worse for a few months more spent on shore if you make good use of your time."

Ned followed his uncle's advice, and did his utmost to overcome his disappointment.

Things went on much as usual at Triton Cottage. Ned frequently got a pull in a revenue boat, but his great delight was to take a sail in one of the fishing crafts belonging to the bay, when the fishermen, with whom he was an especial favourite, gave him instruction in steering and other nautical knowledge, so that he learned how to handle a boat, to furl and shorten sail, to knot and splice, as well as to row.

His uncle always encouraged him to go when the weather was moderate, but on two or three occasions when it came on unexpectedly to blow, and the boats were kept out, poor Aunt Sally was put into a great state of trepidation until he came back safe. Nearly a month had passed since the lieutenant's return home, and no letter had been received either from the Admiralty or from any of the shipowners. The family were seated at tea. The lieutenant could not help occasionally speaking of the subject which occupied his thoughts, generally concluding by saying, "Well, never mind, something may turn up!"

Just then a ring was heard at the door, and Jane put her head in to say that Mr. Hanson had called.

"I'll bring him in to take a cup of tea," said the lieutenant, rising and stumping out of the room. He soon returned with his friend.

"Well, Pack, I've come to wish you and Miss Sarah good-bye," said their guest. "Commander Curtis, an old friend of mine, has been appointed to the 'Ione' corvette, fitting out for the Cape station, and he has applied for me as his first lieutenant. Though I had made up my mind to remain on shore, as he is a man I should like to serve under, I have accepted his offer, and am going off to join the ship as soon as I can be relieved—in two or three days, I hope."

Ned listened, expecting that something else of interest to him was about to follow, but he was disappointed. He was not aware that even a first lieutenant could not obtain a berth for a midshipman.

"Very sorry to lose you, Hanson," said Lieutenant Pack; "you, I daresay will be glad to get afloat again, as there is a better chance of promotion than you would have on shore. We never know what may turn up. We may be at loggerheads with the French, or Russians, or some other people before your commission is over."

Their guest saw Ned looking at him. He divined the boy's thoughts.

"I wish that I had power to take you with me, Ned, but I have not, and I very much fear that the commander will have given away his appointment, and he has but one. However, when I accepted his proposal, I wrote saying that I had a young friend who wished to go to sea, and should be very glad if he would nominate him. I'll let you know as soon as I get his answer, but I do not want unduly to arouse your expectations."

Ned heartily thanked his friend for his good intentions towards him, as did his uncle.

"I knew you would serve him, Hanson, if you could, and if you are not successful, I'll take the will for the deed," said the old lieutenant, as he shook the hand of his guest, whom he accompanied to the door.

Two days afterwards a note came from Lieutenant Hanson, enclosing one from the commander of the " Ione," regretting that he had already filled up his nomination, and had just heard that the Admiralty had already promised the only other vacancy.

" It can't be helped, Ned," said Lieutenant Pack, in a tone which showed how disheartened he was, although he did not intend to exhibit his feelings. " Cheer up, we must not be cast down, we'll still hope that something will turn up. In the meantime we'll try and be as happy as we can. Aunt Sally and Mary are not tired of you, nor am I, my boy. It's only because I know that you wish to be doing something, and that you are right in your wishes, that I regret this delay."

Mary, though sympathising with Ned, could not from her heart say that she was sorry. For the last two days she had been expecting to hear that he would have to go off immediately.

Next morning the postman was seen coming up to the door with an official-looking letter in his hand, and another of ordinary appearance; Ned ran out to receive them. The first was addressed to Lieutenant Pack, R.N. He opened it with far more agitation than he was wont to exhibit. His countenance brightened.

"Ned, my boy!" he exclaimed, "this letter has reference to you. My Lords do recognise my services— it is gratifying, very gratifying—and they have nominated you as a volunteer of the first class to Her Majesty's ship 'Ione,' Commander Curtis, now fitting out at Portsmouth; the very ship of which Hanson is to be first lieutenant. This is fortunate. If he has not started, I'll get him to take you to Portsmouth, and arrange your outfit. He'll do it, I am sure, and will stand your friend if you do your duty; I know that you will do that, and become an honour to the service, as your father would have been had he lived."

Suddenly a thought seemed to strike the lieutenant. He had forgotten a very important matter — the difficulty of obtaining the required funds. The balance at his banker's would not meet the expenses to which he himself must be put, even although the commander might not insist on the usual allowance made to midshipmen. He was silent, thinking of what could be done, and overlooking the envelope which lay on the table beneath the official dispatch.

"Surely there was another letter," remarked Aunt Sally. "I wonder who it can come from?"

"Bless me! so there is," said the lieutenant, glad to have for a moment another occupation for his thoughts. He examined the address, and then the coat of arms on the seal, before breaking it open, which he did deliberately, as if he did not expect to find anything of interest within. His countenance had brightened when he saw the letter from the Admiralty, but it lighted up still more as he read the letter.

"Well, I little expected this from a stranger, at least from one on whom we have no possible claim. Most liberal and generous. I said something would turn up. What do you think, Sally? I really can scarcely read it for the satisfaction it gives me, but I'll try. It begins—

"My dear Friend,—A severe illness has prevented me hitherto from communicating with you, and from the same cause I was unable to attempt forwarding your nephew's views; but as soon as I was well enough I applied to the Admiralty, and their lordships, in consideration of your own and brother-in-law's services, promised to nominate his son to the first ship fitting out. I have to-day heard that he has been appointed to the 'Ione.' As I am aware that his outfit and allowance while at sea will entail certain expenses, I have requested Commander Curtis to draw on my bankers for the latter, while I beg to enclose a cheque for a hundred pounds, which will cover the cost of his outfit, and it will afford me great satisfaction to defray any further expenses which unexpectedly may occur." The letter was signed, "Your faithful and deeply-obliged friend, J. Farrance."

The tears started into Aunt Sally's eyes as she

heard the letter read. They were tears which showed how grateful she felt at the thought of her brother's anxieties being relieved, mingled, however, with the feeling that dear Ned was so soon to leave them.

" How very, very kind of Mr. Farrance to help you to become a midshipman, and some day you may perhaps be made a lieutenant. I am indeed glad ! " exclaimed Mary, though her faltering voice and the tears which filled her eyes belied her words, as she remembered that Ned must go away, and perhaps not come back for many long years.

" This is indeed far better than I could have hoped for," observed the lieutenant, who had been again glancing over the letter while his sister and Mary had been talking.

Ned himself for a minute or more could not utter a word.

" We must lose no time in setting about doing what is necessary," continued the lieutenant. " Sally, you'll get his things ready as fast as you can. He will only require, however, a change or two, to serve him until he can obtain his outfit. I'll write to the Admiralty to say that he will join the ' Ione' forthwith, and to Mr. Farrance to thank him for his generous offer, which I will accept for Ned, although I might have thought twice about it had it been made more directly in my favour. Ned, as soon as you have breakfasted, start away for Longview station. Give Mr. Hanson my regards, and say I shall be grateful to him if he will take you under his wing to Portsmouth, and arrange about your outfit; it will save me the expense of the journey, though I should wonderfully like to see you on board your ship, to introduce you to the captain and your future mess-mates. Sally, give Ned some slices of bread and butter, while Mary pours me out a cup of tea."

Ned having diligently set to work to swallow the food, in less than a minute declared himself ready to start.

"But you have taken nothing, my poor boy!" exclaimed Aunt Sally.

"I can eat the rest on the way," answered Ned, showing a slice of bread which he had doubled up and put into his pocket.

"All right, you'll do well!" said his uncle, nodding approvingly. "When you receive an order, lose no time in executing it."

Ned ran off, sprang up the hill with the agility of a deer, and made his way to the coast-guard station faster than he had ever before performed the distance. Standing at the door he found a stranger, who inquired his errand.

"Mr. Hanson started this morning, or he would have been happy to take charge of you, youngster," was the answer he received. "But my son Charley is to join the 'Ione' in a couple of days, and you can accompany him. As he has been to sea before, he will look after you and keep you out of mischief. Tell your uncle, as

I don't want to bring him all this way, that I will, with his leave, call upon him in the course of the morning to make the necessary arrangements. I'll make you known, however, to my son before you go back ; come in and have some breakfast."

" Thank you, sir, I have already had mine, and my uncle wants me to return as soon as possible ; but I shall be glad to be introduced to your son. Who shall I tell my uncle you are, sir ? "

" Say Lieutenant Meadows ; we were for a short time messmates as midshipmen on board the old ' Goliath,' and I knew his brother-in-law, poor Garth. Was he your father ? "

" Yes, sir," answered Ned.

" I'm very glad that his son and mine are to be together. Charley ! " he shouted, turning round.

At the summons, a fine-looking lad in a midshipman's uniform, about two years older than Ned, made his appearance, his face well bronzed by a tropical sun and sea air. Ned thought at once, from the look he had at his countenance, that he should like him. Lieutenant Meadows introduced the boys to each other, and they shook hands, Charley saying that he should be very glad to be of any service to his future messmate.

Ned, after exchanging a few words, wished his new friends good-bye, and hurried homewards, well pleased at the thoughts of having a companion on his journey who would put him up to what he would have to do on board ship. This would make amends for his

disappointment at not being able to accompany Mr.
Hanson; Ned had not then learned to hold in any
especial awe the first lieutenant of a man-of-war, or
he might greatly have preferred the society of the
midshipman to that of his superior officer.

" I would rather you had been able to accompany
Hanson," observed his uncle, when Ned made his
report. " This youngster may be a very steady fellow,
and do his best to help you, or he may be much the
contrary and try to lead you into all sorts of mischief;
we cannot always judge by the outside appearance.
No, I won't risk it, I'll go with you and take charge
of you both; his father won't object to that. I shall
save Hanson the trouble of getting your outfit—he'll
have quite enough to do—and I'll introduce you to
your commander. Yes, yes, that will be the best
plan."

In the course of the forenoon Lieutenant Meadows
and his son Charley paid their promised visit to Triton
Cottage. The two old shipmates soon recognised each
other, and were well pleased with the anticipation of
having long yarns together about former days. The
visitors were introduced to Aunt Sally and Mary.

The arrangements for the journey were soon concluded, for Mr. Meadows, knowing what youngsters
are made of, was happy to place his son in charge of
a brother officer, who would look after him until he
had joined his new ship.

While Ned was sent out of the room with a message

to Jane and Tom to get luncheon ready, Mary, though somewhat timidly, managed to get near Charley Meadows.

"I want you to be kind to Ned, to take good care of him," she whispered. "You do not know what a good boy he is; and we are very, very sorry for him to go away, though we try to look cheerful, as he wants to become a sailor, and we do not like to prevent him."

"Of course, young lady, for your sake I'll take as much care of him as I can," answered Charley, looking down at Mary's sweet face, as she raised it with an imploring look to his.

"But I want you to take care of him for his own sake, and be a brother to him, for he has no brother of his own, and, except Lieutenant Hanson, who knows him, he will be among strangers."

"Mr. Hanson is first lieutenant of the ship, and will be able to take much better care of him than I can," said Charley, "but I promise you I will look after him and fight for him if necessary; but he seems a young fellow who can stand up for himself, though, as he has not been to sea before, he will be rather green at first."

"Thank you, thank you!" said Mary. "I felt that I must ask you, for you do not know how we all love him."

"He is a fortunate fellow," observed Charley, smiling, "and I daresay he will make friends where-ever he goes; at all events, I promise that I will be his friend if he will let me."

"O yes, I am sure he will; I am so glad that I spoke to you."

"All right, little lady, set your mind at rest on that score," said Charley. "Here comes your brother."

Before Mary could explain that Ned was not her brother (indeed she so completely looked upon him as a brother that she often forgot that he was not so), he entered the room. Mary's heart was greatly relieved at the thoughts that Ned had already found a friend among his future messmates.

CHAPTER V.

TWO days afterwards found the one-legged lieutenant and his young companions on their way to Portsmouth. Ned bore the parting manfully, though he did not the less acutely feel having to wish good-bye to Aunt Sally, Mary, and Tom Baraka.

"If you go to my country, Massa Ned, an' if you see any ob my people, tell dem where Tom Baraka is," said the black, as he wrung Ned's hand. "Dare is one ting I long for—to find my wife and boy, and to tell dem dat I Christian, an' want dem to be Christian also."

"You have not told me your son's name, so that even should I meet him, I should not know that he is your son," said Ned.

"Him called Chando," answered Tom. "Him know dat name when you call him."

"And your wife—what is her name?" asked Ned.

"Him—Masika," said Tom after a few moments' thought—it was so long since he had uttered his wife's name. "O Massa Ned, you bring dem back, and God bless you."

"Chando—Masika," repeated Ned. "But I am afraid that there is very little chance of my finding your family, Tom, though I should be truly thankful to meet with them; I don't know even to what part of the coast of Africa I am going. It is a large country, and though I may see thousands of the inhabitants, those you care for may not be among them."

"Massa Ned, if God wish to bring dem to you, He can find de way," said the black, in a tone of simple faith. "I no say He will do it, but He can do it, dat I know."

Ned did not forget this conversation with poor Tom, not that he entertained the slightest hope that he should fall in with his wife or son; indeed, should he do so, how should he possibly know them? He determined, however, to ask all the Africans he might meet with where they came from, and should it appear that they were natives of the part of the country Tom had described to him, to make more minute inquiries. He knew as well as Tom that God can bring about whatever He thinks fit; but he was too well instructed not to know that our Heavenly Father does not always act as men wish or think best—for that He sees what man in his blindness does not. No one, except Mary, perhaps, missed Ned more than did Tom Baraka. Poor Mary! it was her first great trial in life. She found more difficulty than she had ever

done before in learning her lessons, and she went
about her daily avocations with a far less elastic step
than was her wont. She was too young, however,
to remain long sorrowful, and was as pleased as
ever to accompany Aunt Sally on her rounds among
her poor neighbours.

The travellers reached Portsmouth, and repaired
to the " Blue Posts," the inn at which Mr. Pack had
been accustomed to put up in his younger days.
Next morning he took the two boys on board the
" Ione," which lay alongside the hulk off the dock-
yard. Lieutenant Hanson, who had already joined,
received them in a kind manner, which made Charley
whisper to Ned that they were all right, as it was
clear that their first lieutenant was not one of those
stiff chaps who look as if they had swallowed pokers,
and he hoped that their commander was of the same
character.

Two days passed rapidly away in visiting the
numerous objects of interest to be seen at Portsmouth. Ned's kit was ready, and his uncle finally
took him on board the " Ione," which had cast off
from the hulk, and was getting ready to go out to
Spithead. Ned was introduced to the commander,
who shook his uncle and him by the hand in a
friendly way.

" I hope that the ship will be a happy one," said
Captain Curtis. " It will depend much on his messmates and him whether it is so, and they'll **find**

me ready to serve them if they act as I trust they may."

The next day the "Ione" went out to Spithead, the one-legged lieutenant, by the commander's invitation, being on board. With a beaming eye he watched Ned, who performed various duties in a way which showed that he knew well what he was about.

"He'll do, he'll do," he said to himself more than once. "Meadows, too, seems an active young fellow. Nothing could have turned out better."

At length the moment for parting came. Ned accompanied his uncle down the side, and again and again the kind old lieutenant wrung his hand before he stepped into the wherry which was to carry him to shore. Ned stood watching the boat, thinking of his uncle and his home, until he was recalled to himself by the boatswain's whistle summoning the crew to weigh anchor and make sail. With a fair breeze and all canvas spread, the "Ione" stood out through the Needle Passage on her course down channel. As she came off that part of the coast where his boyhood had been spent, he turned a wistful gaze in that direction, knowing that although the lieutenant was not at home, his telescope would be pointed seaward, and that even then Mary might be looking at the graceful ship which floated like a swan over the calm water. The Lizard was the last point of land seen, and the "Ione" stood out into the broad Atlantic.

" Well, Ned, we are at sea at last , you really have shown yourself more of a man than I expected," said Charley Meadows.

" What should have made you fancy I should have been otherwise ? " asked Ned.

" Why, you 've been brought up so much at home that I was afraid you 'd prove rather too soft for the life you 'll have to lead on board. However, I have no fear about that, whatever others may think. Some of the fellows may try to bully you because you are the youngest on board, but keep your temper, and do not let them see that you know what they are about; I 'll back you up, and they 'll soon cease annoying you."

Ned followed his friend's advice, and managed without quarrelling or fighting to obtain the respect of even the least well-disposed of his messmates.

Charley was at first inclined to exhibit a somewhat patronising manner towards Ned, who, however, wisely did not show that he perceived this, nor did he in the slightest degree resent it. He from the first had endeavoured to gain all the nautical knowledge he possibly could, and was never ashamed of asking for information from those able to afford it.

" That 's the way to become a seaman," observed Mr. Dawes the boatswain, to whom he frequently went when he wanted any matter explained. " Come to me as often as you like, and I shall be glad to tell you what I know; and I ought to know a thing or

two, as I've been at sea, man and boy, pretty near
five-and-twenty years, though I've not got much
book-learning."

Ned thanked him, promising to take advantage of
his offer, and, as was natural, became a great favourite
with the boatswain. . Ned was well up in many of
the details of seamanship, and having been accustomed to boats all his life, was as well able to
manage one as anybody on board.   He quickly
learned to go aloft, and to lay out on the yards to
reef or loose the sails, while he was as active and
fearless as many a far older seaman.   His knowledge
of navigation too was considerable, his uncle having
taken great pains to instruct him, he, on his part,
being always anxious to learn.   Charley, therefore, in
a short time, finding that Ned was not only his
equal in most respects, but his superior in several,
dropped his patronising manner, and they became
faster friends than ever.

The first lieutenant, Mr. Hanson, did not fail to
remark Ned's progress, and calling him up, expressed
his approval.   "Go on as you have begun, Garth,
and you will become a good officer.   The commander
has his eye on you, and will always, you may depend
upon it, prove your friend."

Although with most of his messmates Ned got on
very well, two or three, it was very evident, disliked
him on account of his zeal and good conduct, which
reflected, they might have considered, on their behaviour.

The senior mate in the berth, "Old Rhymer" as he was called, who was soured by disappointment at not obtaining his commission, as he thought he ought to have done long ago, took every opportunity of finding fault with him, and was continually sneering at what he said when at the mess table. If he attempted to reply, O'Connor, the eldest of the midshipmen, was sure to come down on him and join Rhymer.

"You'll be after getting a cobbing, Master Garth, if you don't keep your tongue quiet in presence of your elders," exclaimed the latter.

"I have said nothing to offend any one," said Ned.

"We are the judges of that," replied O'Connor, beginning to knot his handkerchief in an ominous fashion. "You and Meadows are becoming too conceited by half, because the first lieutenant and the commander have taken it into their heads that you are something above the common."

"I have no reason to suppose that from anything they have said to me," answered Ned. "The first lieutenant merely advised me to go on doing my duty, and that is what I intend to do; I don't see how that should offend you."

"We are the best judges of what is offensive and what is not, Master Jackanapes," exclaimed Rhymer, "so take that for daring to reply," and he threw a biscuit across the berth, which would have hit Ned on the eye had he not ducked in time to avoid it.

" Thank you for your good intentions, Rhymer,"
said Ned, picking up the biscuit and continuing to eat
the duff on which he was engaged.

O'Connor meantime went on knotting his handkerchief, and only waiting for a word from Rhymer to
commence operations on Ned's back. Ned took no
notice, but as soon as he had finished dinner he sprang
up and made for the door of the berth.

"Stop that youngster!" exclaimed Rhymer; " he
is not to set our authority at defiance. Come back I
say, Garth."

No one, however, laid a hand on Ned, who, making
his way round on the locker behind his companions'
backs, gained the door. O'Connor, eager to obey the
old mate's commands, made a spring over the table, and
in so doing caught the table-cloth with his foot, and
toppling over on his face, brought it after him with the
plates and other articles to the deck outside the berth,
where he lay struggling, amid shouts of laughter from
his messmates.

Ned reached the upper deck before O'Connor had
regained his legs. The latter was not inclined to
follow him, though he vowed he would be revenged on
the first opportunity. Ned was soon joined by Charley
Meadows.

" You have made enemies of those two fellows, and
they 'll pay you off some day," observed Charley.

" I am sorry for that, though I do not fear
their enmity, and I will try and make friends with

them as soon as possible," answered Ned. He watched for an opportunity, and was careful not to say anything in the berth likely to offend his elders. Notwithstanding, they continued to treat him much in the same way, though O'Connor forbore the use of the cob, as he had promised, finding that public opinion was decidedly against him.

Week after week went by, the "Ione" steadily continuing her course to the southward. A heavy gale came on, which, though it lasted but a few days, served to show that Ned was not only a fair-weather sailor, but could do his duty in foul weather as well as in fine. Then there were calms and light winds.

The line was passed. Much to O'Connor's disappointment, the commander would not allow the usual customs, having given notice that he should not receive " Daddy Neptune " and his Tritons on board.

The ship put into Rio, in South America, which, though apparently out of her course, was not really so. Having remained a few days in that magnificent harbour, and obtained a supply of fresh provisions and water, she again sailed, and soon fell in with the south-easterly trade wind, which carried her rapidly without a tack across the Atlantic. Table Bay was soon reached, and the officers were anticipating a run on shore, when the commander received orders to sail immediately for the east coast, to assist in putting a stop to the trade in slaves, said to be carried on along it for the supply of the Persian and Arabian markets.

Many of the mess grumbled at being sent off so soon again to sea, and declared that they would have remained on shore had they known they were to be engaged in such abominable work.

" I have heard all about it," exclaimed Rhymer. "We shall never have a moment's quiet, but be chasing those Arab dhows night and day, and if we capture any, have to crowd up our decks with hundreds of dirty blackamoors, whom we shall be obliged to nurse and feed until we can set them on shore, with the chances of fever or small-pox and all sorts of complaints breaking out among them."

Very different were Ned's feelings when he heard the news; it was the very station to which he had hoped the ship might be sent. His knowledge of the good qualities possessed by Tom Baraka made him sure that the blacks were not the despicable race some of his messmates were disposed to consider them. They, at all events, had immortal souls, and might with the same advantages become as civilised and as good a Christian as Tom was. There was a possibility, though a very remote one, that he might fall in with Tom's wife and child, and he pictured to himself the satisfaction of being able to restore them to liberty. He did not, however, express his feelings, except to Charley, as he considered, justly, that it would be like throwing pearls before swine to say anything of the sort to Rhymer or O'Connor, who would only have laughed at him.

The " Ione " had a quick passage round the south coast of Africa, and she now entered the Mozambique Channel. The chart showed that she had reached the twentieth degree of south latitude, and about the forty-first of east longitude. Away to the west, though far out of sight, were the mouths of the Zambesi river, whose waters have been explored from their source to the ocean by the energetic Livingstone, while to the right was the magnificent island of Madagascar, many of whose long benighted people have since accepted the Gospel. The ship glided on over the smooth sea, her sails spread to a gentle southerly breeze. The heat was great ; it had been rapidly increasing. As the hot sun shone down from a cloudless sky on the deck, the pitch bubbled up as if a fire were beneath it, and O'Connor declared that he could cook a beef steak, if he had one, on the capstan head.

" Hot, do you call it ? " observed Rhymer, who had before been in those seas. " Wait until we get under the line ; we may roast an ox there by tricing it up to the fore-yard, and even then should have to lower it into the sea every now and then to prevent it being done too quickly."

Every shady spot was eagerly sought for by officers and crew, though, as the air was pure, no one really suffered by the heat. Other smaller islands were passed, though not seen—among them Johanna and Comoro, inhabited by dark-skinned races. At last the island of Zanzibar, close in with the African coast, was sighted, and as the breeze blew off its undulating plains, Ned and Charley agreed that they could inhale the perfume of its spice groves and its many fragrant flowers. As the ship drew nearer the land, on the lower ground could be distinguished large plantations of sugar-cane, with forests of cocoa-nut trees, just beyond the line of shining sands separating them from the blue water, while here and there rose low rocky cliffs of varied tints of red and brown. On the uplands were seen rows of clove-trees ranged in exact order between the plantations, groups of palm or dark-leaved mangoes, with masses of wild jungle, where nature was still allowed to have its own way. Further on white flat-roofed buildings with numerous windows appeared in sight; then the har-bour opened up, in which floated a crowd of vessels of all nations, some with red banners floating from their mast-heads, forming the sultan's navy, others English ships of war, merchantmen, countless dhows with high sterns and strange rigs; then more houses and terraces with arches and colonnades came into view, with several consular flags flying above them.

"That's Zanzibar, the capital of the sultan of that ilk. A very beautiful place you may think it," said Rhymer; "but wait until we get on shore, and then give me your opinion."

"Shorten sail and bring ship to an anchor!" shouted the first lieutenant.

The boatswain's whistle sounded, the hands flew

aloft, the canvas was furled, and in a few minutes the "Ione" was brought up at no great distance from the town. The commander shortly afterwards went on shore, and several members of the midshipmen's berth obtained leave to follow him under charge of Rhymer.

"Remember, young gentlemen, keep together, and do nothing to offend the natives," said Mr. Hanson as they were about to shove off. "They are not like the inhabitants of European places, and are quick to resent what they may consider an insult. You cannot be too careful in your conduct towards them."

Attractive as the place appeared from the sea, the party had not gone far when they were inclined to pass a very different opinion on it. The houses looked dilapidated, the inhabitants, black and brown, squalid and dirty, though a few Arabs in picturesque costumes, armed to the teeth, were encountered strolling about with a swaggering air, while odours abominable in the extreme rose from all directions. The party made their way through the crooked, narrow lanes, with plastered houses on each side, in the lower floors of which were Banyans, wearing red turbans, seated in front of their goods, consisting either of coloured cottons or calicoes, or heaps of ivory tusks, or of piles of loose cotton, crockery, or cheap Birmingham ware. Further on they came to rows of miserable huts, the doors occupied by woolly-headed blacks, who, in spite of the filth and offensive smells arising from heaps of refuse, seemed as merry as crickets, laughing, chattering, and bargaining in loud tones.

Most of the people they met on foot appeared to be bending their steps to one quarter; on pursuing the same road the naval party found themselves at the entrance of a large open space or square crowded with people. Round it were arranged groups of men, women, and children of various hues, jet black or darkest of browns predominating.

"Who can all these people be?" asked Charley.

"Slaves, to be sure; they are brought here to be sold," answered Rhymer. "Let's go on, it will be some fun to watch them."

Rhymer led the way round the square, examining the different groups of slaves. Although the greater number looked very squalid and wretched, others had evidently been taken care of. Among them were a party of Gallas, mostly women, habited in silk and gauze dresses, with their hair prettily ornamented to increase their personal attractions, which were far superior to those of the negroes. Close to the group stood a man who acted as auctioneer, ready to hand his goods over to the highest bidder. The purchasers were chiefly Arabs, who walked about surveying the hapless slaves, and ordering those to whom they took a fancy to be paraded out before them, after which they examined the mouths and limbs of any they thought of purchasing, striking their breasts and pinching their arms and legs to ascertain that

they possessed sufficient muscle and wind for their
work.

Ned turned away from the scene with disgust. He
longed to be able to liberate the poor slaves, and to
place them where they could obtain religious instruction and the advantages of civilisation, for they
were, he knew, being dragged from one state of
barbarism to another, in many cases infinitely worse,
where they would become utterly degraded and
debased.

"Is there no hope for these poor people?" he
exclaimed, turning to Charley. "Cannot our commander interfere?"

"He has not the authority to do so in the
dominions of the sultan; we can only touch those
whom we meet on the high seas, beyond certain limits.
We shall soon have an opportunity, however, of
setting some of them free, for the commander told
Mr. Hanson that we are only to remain here a couple
of days, and then to commence our cruise to the
northward."

"The sooner the better," exclaimed Ned; "we
shall all catch fever if we stay long in this place.
Rhymer was right in what he said about it, fair as it
looks outside."

Ned was not disappointed; the "Ione" was soon
again at sea, and had reached the latitude beyond
which his commander had authority to capture all
dhows with slaves on board. A bright look-out was

kept aloft, from the first break of day until darkness covered the face of the deep, for any dhows sailing northward, but day after day passed by and none were seen. The ship was then kept further off the land, the commander suspecting that the Arabs and slave traders had notice of his whereabouts. The following day three dhows were seen ; chase was made ; they were overtaken and boarded ; one, however, was a fair trader, but about the two others there was considerable doubt. They each carried a large number of people, whom the Arab captains averred were either passengers or part of their crews. As no one contradicted them, they were allowed to proceed on their voyage.

"This dhow chasing is dull work," exclaimed Rhymer. "I'll bet anything that we don't make a single capture ; and if we do, what is the good of it, except the modicum of prize money we might chance to pocket ? The blacks won't be a bit the better off, and the Arabs will be the losers."

"They deserve to be the losers," exclaimed Charley, who, influenced by the remarks of Ned, had become as much interested as he was in the duty in which they were engaged. "What business have they to make slaves of their fellow-creatures?"

"Business! Why, because they want slaves, and set about the best way of getting them," answered Rhymer, with a laugh.

The ship was now nearly under the line. The heat,

as Rhymer had forewarned his messmates, was very great, though not enough to roast an ox; and when there was a breeze, it was at all events endurable in the shade. Had it been much greater it would not have impeded Commander Curtis in the performance of his duty. Ned bore it very well, although he confessed to Charley that he should like a roll in the snow. When the ship was becalmed the crew were allowed a plunge overboard, but they were ordered to keep close to the side for fear of sharks, and a sail was rigged out in the water for those who could not swim. Several more days passed without a single dhow being seen, and Rhymer declared that they would catch no slavers, for the best of reasons, that there were no slavers to be caught, or that if there were, they would take good care to keep out of their way.

CHAPTER VI.

T was Ned's morning watch. Scarcely had the first streaks of crimson and gold appeared in the eastern sky, heralding the coming day, than the look-out, who had just reached the mast-head, shouted—

"Three sail on the port bow," and presently afterwards he announced two more in the same direction. The wind was southerly and light, the ship's head was to the northward. The commander, according to his orders, was immediately called. All hands were roused up to make sail, and soon every stitch of canvas the ship could carry being packed on her, the foam which bubbled up under her bows showed that she was making good way in the direction in which the strangers had been seen. As soon as Ned was able, he hurried aloft with his spy-glass, eager to have a look at them. He counted not only five, but six, all of them dhows. As yet they were probably not aware of the presence of a man-of-war, for their hulls were still below the horizon. He hoped, therefore, that the "Ione" would gain on them before they should hoist their larger sails. He knew that it was the custom of the Arabs to carry only small sails at night. The usual preparations were made on board the corvette, the boats were cleared ready for lowering, the bow-chasers loaded and run out, and buckets of water were thrown over the sails to make them hold the wind.

"We are gaining on them!" exclaimed Ned to Charley, as, after a third trip aloft, he came again on deck.

"So we may be, but we must remember that after all they may be only honest traders, and not have a slave on board," observed Charley. "We shall judge better if they make more sail when they discover us. If they are honest traders they will keep jogging on as before, if not, depend upon it they will try to escape."

"They may try, but they'll find that the 'Ione' has a fast pair of heels, and we shall have the fun of overhauling them at all events," said Ned.

At length the Arabs must have discovered the man-of-war. First the nearest hoisted her big sail, and also set one on her after-mast. Then another and another dhow followed her example, and then the whole squadron, like white-winged birds, went skimming along over the blue sea.

"What do you think now, Charley, of the strangers?" asked Ned.

"No doubt that they wish to keep ahead of us, but whether or not we shall get up with them is another question, though, if the wind holds as it now does, we may do it."

The commander and gun-room officers were fully as eager as Ned to overtake the dhows. They had, they thought, at length got some veritable slavers in sight, and it would be provoking to lose them. It was, however, curious that they should all keep together; probably, however, none of them wished to steer a course by which they would run a greater chance of falling into the power of their pursuer. Seldom had breakfast been disposed of more quickly by officers and crew than that morning. The dhows could now be seen clearly from the deck, proof positive that the corvette was sailing much faster than they were. Once headed, most of them might be captured, for the dhow can sail but badly on a wind, though no vessel is faster before it.

The lofty canvas of the corvette gave her an advantage over the dhows, whose sails occasionally hung down from their yards, almost emptied of wind.

" We shall soon get them within range of our long gun," said the commander, as he stood eagerly watching the vessels ahead. "Stand by, Mr. Hanson, to lower the boats; we shall be able to do so with this breeze without heaving to."

"Is the gun all ready forward?" he asked a few minutes later.

"Aye, aye, sir," was the answer.

His practised eye assured him that the sterrmost dhow was within range of the long gun.

"We'll make that fellow lower his canvas, and then see what cargo he carries," said the commander. "Send a shot across his forefoot, and if that doesn't stop him we'll try to knock away that big yard of his. All ready there forward?"

"Aye, aye, sir!"

"Fire!"

The missile flew from the mouth of the gun, and was seen to strike the surface so close to the dhow as to send the spray over her low bows. Still she held on her course. The gun was run in and reloaded.

"Give her another shot!" cried the commander; "and if they don't bring to, the Arabs must take the consequences."

The second lieutenant, who had been carefully taking the range, obeyed the order. The shot was seen to touch the water twice before it disappeared, but whether it struck the dhow seemed doubtful. Again the gun was got ready, but this time was aimed at the next vessel ahead, which almost immediately lowered her sails, the one astern following her example.

"Let Mr. Rhymer, with a midshipman, shove off and take possession of those two vessels, while we stand after the others. We must try and bag the whole of them, for I suspect they all have slaves on board," observed the commander.

" Garth, do you accompany Rhymer," said Mr.
Hanson. " Take care that the Arabs don't play you
any trick."

The ship was moving so steadily over the smooth
water that there was no necessity to stop her way,
though even then it required care in lowering the boat.
The crew with the two young officers were soon in her,
the oars were got out, and away she pulled after the
sternmost dhow, while the ship stood on in chase of
the remainder of the fleet. The crew of the boat gave
way, eager to secure their prize. Scarcely, however,
had they got half-way to the nearest, than the breeze
freshened up again, and the corvette's speed was so
increased, that it would have now been no easy task to
lower a boat. They were soon up to the dhow, on
board of which there appeared to be a crew of from
fifteen to twenty Arabs, who gazed with folded arms and
scowling countenances on their approaching captors.
Rhymer and Ned sprang on board. No resistance was
offered. The Arab captain shrugged his shoulders, said
something, which probably meant, " It is the fortune
of war," and appeared perfectly resigned to his fate.
A peep down the main hatchway showed at once that
she was a slaver, as the bamboo deck was crowded
with blacks, who commenced shrieking fearfully as they
saw Ned's white face, having been told by the Arabs
that the object of the English was to cook and eat them.

" Stop those fellows from making that horrible
uproar," cried Rhymer in an angry tone. " I cannot

make out what these Arabs say with this abominable noise."

It is very doubtful if he would have understood his prisoners even had there been perfect silence. In order not to be seen by the blacks Ned walked aft.

Rhymer made signs to the Arabs to give up their arms, which he handed into the boat as the best means of preventing any attempt they might make to recapture their vessel. He then ordered them to go forward to rehoist the sail, while he sent one of his men to the helm.

While they were engaged in these arrangements, Ned cast his eye on the other dhow, of which Rhymer had been ordered to take charge.

"Look out there, Rhymer!" he exclaimed; "that fellow is getting up his long yard again, and will try to give us the slip."

"We'll soon stop him from doing that," answered Rhymer. "You remain on board this craft with a couple of hands and I'll go after him. Cox and Stone, you stay with Mr. Garth; into the boat the rest of you." The crew in another instant were in their seats, and shoving off, pulled away towards the other dhow. There was no time to lose, for already the yard with its white canvas was half way up the mast. The breeze, too, was freshening, and as Ned watched her it seemed to him that she had a good chance of escaping. The boat's crew were pulling as hard as they could lay their backs to the oars. He saw Rhymer standing up with a musket in his hand, and shouting to the Arabs, threatening to fire should they continue the attempt to escape. They were, however, apparently not to be deterred from so doing. Still the sail continued to ascend and the dhow was gathering way. Should the sail once be got up, the boat would have little chance of catching her. Rhymer, however, was not likely to give up the pursuit. Finding that his threats were not attended to, he fired one of the muskets, but whether any person was hit Ned could not discover. Again Rhymer fired, and then reloaded both muskets. Ned was so engaged in watching the boat, that he scarcely took notice of the proceedings of the Arabs on board his own dhow. He observed, however, that one of them, a young man with a better-looking countenance than most of his companions, had remained aft, while the rest were attempting to hoist the sail, though from some cause or other the halyards appeared to have got foul.

" Go forward, Cox, and see what those fellows are about," he said; " I 'll take the helm."

The seaman obeyed, while Stone, beckoning to the young Arab to come to his assistance, stood by to haul in the main sheet. The only thing in the shape of a boat was a small canoe which lay in the after part of the vessel. Aided by Cox, the sail was soon hoisted, but scarcely had the dhow heeled over to the breeze, than cries arose from the Arab crew, who made frantic gesticulations, indicating that the vessel was sinking. Ned at once suspected the cause; their second shot must have struck the bows of the dhow between wind and water, and had probably started a plank, so as to allow the sea, like a mill stream, to rush into her. There was little hope of stopping it. Ned put up the helm. " Lower the sail ! " he shouted as he had never shouted before ; the seamen endeavoured to obey the order, but the halyards had again become jammed, and to his dismay he saw that the bows of the dhow were rapidly sinking. As the water rushed into the hold the poor blacks uttered the most piercing shrieks, while the panic-stricken Arabs in a body frantically sprang towards the after part of the vessel ; but as they came along, the light deck gave way beneath their weight, and the whole of them were precipitated on to the heads of the hapless negroes below.

" We must save ourselves, sir," cried Stone, lifting the canoe. " It is our only chance, or we shall be drowned with the rest."

" Where is Cox ? " exclaimed Ned.

He had fallen in among the struggling Arabs and blacks. Ned caught sight of him for a moment, and was springing forward to help him out from their midst, when the stern of the dhow lifted. Stone launched the canoe and leaped into her, shouting to his young officer to join him, while he paddled with a piece of board clear of the sinking vessel. Ned seeing that Cox had managed to reach the side, sprang overboard, his example being followed by the latter, as well as by the young Arab who had remained aft. Before any of the rest of the crew had extricated themselves, the dhow, plunging her head into the sea, rapidly glided downwards, and in an instant the despairing cries of the perishing wretches which had filled the air were silenced. Stone, influenced by the natural desire of saving his own life, paddled away with might and main to escape being drawn down in the vortex. Ned had also struck out bravely, though he had to exert all his swimming powers to escape. For an instant he cast a glance back; the dhow had disappeared with all those on board; Cox was nowhere to be seen; he caught sight, however, of the young Arab, who, having clutched hold of a piece of bamboo, had come to the surface, but was evidently no swimmer.

"I must try and save that poor fellow," he thought. "I can manage to keep him afloat until the canoe gets up to us." Ned carried out his intention. On reaching the young Arab he made a sign to him to turn on his back, placing the piece of bamboo under him. Just then he heard a faint shout—it came from Cox, who had returned to the surface, though, like the Arab, unable to swim.

"Save me, save me!" shouted Cox, who was clinging to a log of wood.

Stone heard him, and Ned saw the head of the

canoe turned towards where the seaman was struggling.

"Pick him up first!" he shouted to Stone. "I
can keep this man afloat until you come to us."

With only a board to impel the canoe, it took
Stone a considerable time to reach his messmate,
whom it was then no easy matter to get into the canoe
without upsetting her. While Stone was thus employed, Ned did his uttermost to calm the fears of
the young Arab, who, besides being unable to swim,
probably recollected that sharks abounded in those
seas, and dreaded lest he and the Englishman might
be attacked by one. Ned thought only of one thing,
that he had to keep himself and a fellow-creature
afloat until the canoe should come up to them. As
to how they should get on board, he did not allow
himself to think just then. She was scarcely large
enough to hold four people, though she might possibly support the whole party until Rhymer could
send the boat to pick them up. Ned, withdrawing
his eyes from poor Cox, who was clinging to his log,
and shouting to his messmate to make haste, looked
towards the dhow of which Rhymer was in chase.
She had hoisted her sail, and should the breeze continue, would very probably get away, unless Rhymer,
by killing or wounding some of her crew, could make
the others give in. He, it was pretty clear, was so
eagerly engaged in pursuing the chase, that he had
not seen the dhow go down. The boat's crew, how-

ever, must have perceived what had happened; and Ned thought it strange that he did not at once return to try and save him and his two men.

"Perhaps he fancies that we are all lost, and that there would be no use in coming to look after us. If he catches the dhow, however, I hope that he will send back the boat, on the chance of any of us having escaped," thought Ned. He could see the sails of the corvette, and an occasional shot told him that she was still firing at the slavers. She was already almost hull down, and the catastrophe could not have been discovered from her deck, while the eyes of the look-outs aloft were probably fixed on the dhows still trying to escape. Still Ned did not give up hopes of being rescued, but continued energetically treading water, and speaking in as cheerful a tone as he could command to keep up the spirits of the young Arab.

"Me understand, t'ankee, t'ankee," said the latter at last.

Still Stone could make but slow progress, and Ned began to fear that his own strength might become exhausted before the canoe could reach him. He was truly thankful when at last he saw that Stone had got hold of Cox, and was dragging him on board. Just at that momemt, however, to his horror, he caught sight of a dark fin above the surface; that it was that of a shark he knew too well. He must do his utmost to keep the monster at a distance. He shouted, and splashed the water with his disengaged hand

"Be quick, be quick, Stone!" he cried. "Do you see that brute?"

"Aye, aye, sir, I see him; but he 'll not come nigh you while you 're splashing about, and the canoe is too big a morsel for him to attack. Now, Ben," he cried, turning to his messmate, "haul yourself on board while I keep at the other end of the canoe, it is the safest plan."

But poor Cox was too much exhausted by his violent struggles to do as he was advised, and at last Stone had to help him, at the risk of upsetting the canoe or bringing her bow under the water. By lying flat along he succeeded, however, at last in hauling his shipmate's shoulders over the bows. He then returned to the stern, when Ben, by great exertion, managed to drag himself in. This done, Stone endeavoured as fast as he could to get up to Ned. As Stone paddled, he sung out, "I 'm afraid it 's of no use trying to keep that Arab fellow above water; you must let him go, for the canoe won't hold us all."

"Not while I have life and strength to help him," answered Ned. "Do not be afraid," he added, turning to the Arab, who understood what Stone had said. "The canoe may support us even though she is brought down to the gunwale; and if she can't, I 'll keep outside and hold on until Mr. Rhymer's boat comes back, or the corvette sends to look for us."

"But the shark!" cried Stone; "the brute may be grabbing you if you remain quiet even for a minute."

"I don't intend to remain quiet," said Ned. "Here, lift the Arab in. I'll help you—it can be done." There certainly was a great risk of the canoe upsetting in doing as Ned proposed. Cox, however, leaned over on the opposite side, and they at length succeeded in getting the Arab on board. The gunwale of the canoe was scarcely a couple of inches above the water; a slight ripple would have filled her, but the sea was so smooth that there was no fear of that happening. Ned, directing the men how to place themselves, was at last drawn safely on board. His additional weight brought the canoe almost flush with the water. They were, however, certainly better off in her than in the water; but at any moment, with the slightest increase of wind, she might fill and sink beneath them, and they would again be left to struggle for their lives. Ned was afraid of moving, and urged his companions to remain perfectly still.

"Look out, Stone; what is the dhow about? Mr. Rhymer will surely soon be sending the boat to our relief—he must have seen our craft go down."

"Not so sure of that; he'll not trouble himself about us," muttered Stone. "If you were there, you'd do it; all officers are not alike."

Ned was afraid that the seaman might be right, but he did not express an opinion on the subject. Their position was, indeed, a trying one. The sun struck down with intense heat on their heads, while they had not a particle of food to satisfy their hunger, nor a drop of fresh water to quench their burning thirst. The breeze had sprung up, and every now and then a ripple broke over the gunwale, even though Stone kept the canoe before the wind.

"If we had a couple of paddles, we might gain on the corvette; but I'm afraid of using this bit of board, for fear of taking the water in on one side or the other," said Stone.

"Do not attempt it," answered Ned; "we should not overtake her unless it should fall calm again, and the commander will surely come and look for us."

"Provided Mr. Rhymer doesn't tell him we are all lost," remarked Stone, who had evidently little confidence in the old mate.

Hour after hour went by, the boat was nowhere to be seen, and the dhows' sails had sunk beneath the horizon. Night was approaching, and as far as the occupants of the canoe could judge, no help was at hand. Ned endeavoured, as well as he could, to keep up the spirits of his companions.

The wind remained light, and the sea was as smooth as a mill-pond. The approaching darkness so far brought relief that they were no longer exposed to the burning rays of the sun, while the cooler air of night greatly relieved them. As the day had passed by, so it appeared probable would the night, without bringing them succour. Ben and the Arab slept, but Ned was too anxious to close his eyes, and Stone insisted on keeping a look-out, on the chance of any vessel passing which might take them on board. Even an Arab dhow would be welcome, for the Arabs would doubtless be willing to receive them on board for the sake of obtaining a reward for preserving their lives. At last the Arab, whose head was resting on Ned's side, awoke. He appeared to be in a very weak state, and told Ned, in his broken English, that he thought he was dying.

" Try and keep alive until to-morrow morning," said Ned; " by that time our ship will be looking for us, and as they know where we were left, we are sure to be seen."

Ned had been calculating that it was about two hours to dawn, when, in spite of his efforts to keep awake, he found his head dropping back on Ben's legs, and he was soon fast asleep. How long he had been lost in forgetfulness he could not tell, when he heard Stone give a loud hail.

" What is that ? " asked Ned, lifting up his head.

" I heard voices and a splash of oars, sir," he answered; " they were a long way off, and, I fancied, passed to the southward."

" Silence, then," said Ned; " we will listen for their reply."

No answering hail came, and he feared that Stone must have been mistaken; again he listened. " Yes, those were human voices and the dip of oars in the water. We'll shout together. Rouse yourself, Cox," he said.

Ben sat up, and, Stone leading, they shouted together at the top of their voices, the young Arab joining them. Again they were silent, but no answer came. "If that is a boat, they surely must have heard us," observed Ned.

"They may be talking themselves, sir, or the noise of their oars prevented them," remarked Stone.

"We'll shout again, then," said Ned.

Again they shouted, this time louder than before. They waited a few seconds, almost afraid to breathe, and then there came across the water a British cheer, sounding faintly in the distance.

"Hurrah! hurrah! All right, sir!" cried Stone. They shouted several times after this to guide the boat towards them. At length they could see her emerging from the gloom; but no one on board her had apparently seen the canoe, for, from the speed the boat was going and the course she was steering, she was evidently about to pass them.

"Boat ahoy!" shouted Stone. "Here we are, but take care not to run us down."

The boat's course was altered; they soon heard a voice, it was that of Charley Meadows, crying out, "There is something floating ahead of us, a raft or a sunken boat."

"Meadows ahoy!" hailed Ned. "Come carefully alongside." The oars were thrown in, and the boat glided up to the canoe.

"Why, Ned, Ned! I am so thankful that I have

found you," cried Charley, as he grasped the hand of his messmate after he had been helped on board.

" There is a poor Arab, take care of him, for he is pretty far gone already," said Ned.

" Water, water," murmured the Arab faintly.

There was fortunately a braker in the boat, and before many words were exchanged some of the refreshing liquid was served out to Ned and his companions. Except a few biscuits there was nothing to eat, but even these soaked in water served to refresh the well-nigh famished party.

Charley then explained that the corvette, having captured three of the dhows, all with slaves on board, had hove to for the purpose of transferring their cargoes to her deck; and that while so occupied, Rhymer had arrived with a fourth, several of the Arab crew having been wounded in attempting to get away. " The commander seeing you were not on board, inquired what had become of you, when Rhymer, with very little concern, replied that he feared you all had gone to the bottom with the dhow, as his boat's crew asserted that they had seen her founder. The commander was very indignant at his not having gone back at once to try and pick you up, should you by any means have escaped. He immediately ordered off three boats—the second lieutenant going in one, Rhymer in another, while he gave me charge of the third. What has become of the other two boats I do not know; perhaps they thought that they had come far enough and have gone back, as I confess I was on the point of doing when I heard your hail. We shall soon, I hope, fall in with the ship, for she is sure to beat back over the ground until she has picked us up."

" I shall be thankful to get on board for the sake of this poor Arab, who requires the doctor's care," said Ned.

" Why, isn't he one of the slaver's crew? " exclaimed Charley. " An arrant rogue, I dare say."

" I don't know about that, but I saved his life," answered Ned, "and I feel an interest in him; he seems grateful too, as far as I can judge."

He then asked the Arab, who was sitting near him, whether he would have some more water, and handed him the cup, which was full.

" T'ankee, t'ankee! " answered the Arab; " much t'ankee! " Ned then gave him some more sopped biscuit.

" What's his name? " inquired Charley. " Ask him, as he seems to speak English."

" Sayd," answered the Arab immediately, showing that he understood what was said.

Charley was now steering the boat to the north-ward. In a short time day broke, and as the sun rose, his rays fell on the white canvas of the corvette, which was standing close-hauled to the south-west, her black hull just seen above the horizon.

" Hurrah! " cried Charley, " there's the old 'barky'; I hope we shall soon be on board."

"If she stands on that course she'll pass us," said Ned.

"No fear of that," answered Charley; "she'll soon be about, and we shall be on board and all to rights."

He was not mistaken; the corvette immediately tacked, her canvas, which had hitherto seemed of snowy whiteness, being thrown into dark shadow. She now stood towards the south-east, on a course which would bring her so near that the boat would soon be seen from her deck. Before long she again came to the wind.

"She is going about again!" exclaimed Ned.

"No, no, she's heaving to to pick up one of the boats," answered Charley.

He was again right; in a few minutes the sails were once more filled, and she stood on. The wind being light, the midshipmen had to wait for some time before they were certain that the boat was seen. The corvette again appeared as if about to pass them, but soon put about, and in less than a quarter of an hour she hove to, to enable Charley to steer alongside.

"Hurrah!" he shouted as he approached, "we have them all safe."

A cheer rose from the throats of the crew as they received this announcement. Ned with his companions were assisted up the side. As he passed along the gangway he observed the unusual appearance which the deck presented, covered as it was by an almost countless number of black figures, men, women, and children, most of them squatting down in the attitudes they had been compelled to preserve on board the slave vessels. He had, however, to make his way aft to the commander, who put out his hand and cordially congratulated him on his escape.

Ned having reported what had happened to him self, added, "There's a poor Arab with me, sir, who requires to be looked after by the doctor. He seems grateful to me for having kept him afloat until the canoe picked us up."

"In other words you saved his life, Garth, at the peril of your own, as far as I can understand. The surgeon will attend to him; and I hope the risk he has run of losing his life will induce him to give up slave-trading for the future. Now, my lad, you must turn into your hammock, you look as if you required rest."

Ned confessed that such was the case, but hinted that he and Sayd would first of all be glad of some food. This was soon brought him, and scarcely a minute had passed after he had tumbled into his hammock before he was fast asleep.

CHAPTER VII.

NED was allowed to take as long a rest as he liked, and it was not until hammocks were piped up the next morning that he awoke. Scarcely had he reached the deck when Sayd, who immeately knew him, hurried up, and making a profound salaam, pressed his hand, and in his broken English warmly thanked him for saving his life.

"I am very glad to have done so," said Ned; "and, as the commander says, the best way you can show your gratitude is to give up slave-dealing for the future, and turn honest trader."

The young Arab evidently did not understand the meaning of what Ned had said, possibly had he done so he would have declared that he was merely following an occupation which his people considered perfectly lawful, and that he saw no reason why he should abandon it. Although he could not exchange many words, Ned felt greatly drawn towards his new friend. There was something very pleasing in the young

Arab's manner; indeed, in every sense of the word, he appeared to be a gentleman. Ned, however, had his duties to perform, and could not just then hold much conversation with him. Both officers and crew were occupied from morning till night in attending to the liberated slaves, who had in the first place to be washed from the filth in which they had lived on board the dhows; they had then to be fed, and most of them also had to be clothed, while constant attention was required to keep each gang on the part of the deck allotted to it. Ned, on inquiring for the dhows, found that all those captured had been destroyed, with the exception of one, on board which the Arab crews had been placed, and allowed to go about their business, as it would have been inconvenient to keep them on board until they could be carried to Aden or Zanzibar.

The ship was now steering for the Seychelles Islands, the nearest place at which negroes could be landed without the risk of again being enslaved. There were upwards of three hundred of these poor creatures on board, of all tints, from yellow and brown to ebon black. Some few, chiefly Gallas, were fine-looking people, with nothing of the negro in their features, and of a dark copper colour; but the greater number, according to European notions, were excessively ugly specimens of the human race. Many were in a deplorable condition, having been long crammed together on the bamboo decks of the dhow,

without being even able to sit upright. Several of
the women had infants in their arms, the poor little
creatures being mere living skeletons; not a few of
them, indeed, died as they were being removed from
the slavers to the ship. Most of the slaves, both men
and women, looked wretched in the extreme, for the
only food they had received for many weeks was a
handful of rice and half a cocoanut full of water.
On board two of the captured dhows not more than
three bags of grain were found to feed between eighty
and a hundred people. At first the poor creatures,
when placed on the man-of-war's deck, looked terrified
in the extreme, but the kindness they received from
the officers and seamen soon reassured them. The
rough "tars" at all hours of the day might be seen
nursing the babies or tending the sick, lifting those
unable to walk from place to place, or carrying them
their food. Not a grumble was heard among the
crew, although their patience was severely taxed.
The provisions, consisting of grain and rice, having
been boiled in the ship's coppers, were served out at
stated times in large bowls to the different messes.
As soon as the food was cooked, the seamen told off
for the purpose came along the deck with the huge
bowls in their hands, one of which was placed in the
midst of each tribe, or gang, of blacks, who lost no
time in falling to, using their fingers to transfer the
hot food to their mouths, often squabbling among
each other when any one was supposed to take more

than his or her share. Ned was as active as any one in tending the poor Africans, much to the astonishment of Sayd, who could not understand why white men should interest themselves about a set of wretched savages, as he considered them. Ned tried to explain that, as they had souls, it was the duty of Christian men to try and improve their condition, and that no people had a right to enslave their fellow-creatures; but though Sayd was intelligent enough about most matters, he failed to understand Ned's arguments, and evidently retained his own opinion to the last. Notwithstanding this, their friendship continued. Ned took great pains to teach Sayd English, which he appeared especially anxious to learn.

With the assistance of the Arab, he made inquiries among all the negroes in the hopes of hearing something about Tom Baraka's family, but nothing could he learn which could lead him to suppose that any one on board was acquainted with them. Even Charley was almost as anxious as he was on the subject, though he owned that he had little hope of success.

"You might as well try to find a needle in a bundle of hay," he observed.

Sayd, too, assured him that so many thousands had been carried off from their families, it would be scarcely possible to identify Baraka's wife and child.

Happily the sea was smooth and the wind

moderate, for had bad weather come on, the sufferings of the slaves would have been greatly increased. At length Mahe, the largest of the Seychelles group, appeared ahead, and a pilot coming on board, the " Ione " brought up in Port Victoria. Everywhere on shore the most beautiful tropical vegetation was seen; the hills covered to their summits with trees, cottages and plantations on the more level ground, while here and there bright coloured cliffs peeped out amid the green foliage. Mahe was pronounced to be a very pretty island indeed, and although so close under the line, it is considered an extremely healthy one.

The slaves were landed, some of them being hired by the planters, while others set up for themselves on ground allotted to them by the government. Before leaving the Seychelles, Commander Curtis had the satisfaction of seeing the larger number of emancipated negroes comfortably settled, and several having agreed to keep house together were legally married. In most respects, after all their troubles, they were far better off than they would have been in their own country, as they were free from the attacks of hostile tribes or wild animals, and ran no risk of again being carried off by Arab slave dealers.

Once more the " Ione " was at sea, and steering so as to cross the track of the slavers. Several dhows were seen, but being to leeward, effected their

escape. Others which came in sight to the southward were compelled to heave to, and were boarded,
but these turned out to be legal traders. Though
many had blacks on board, it could not be proved
that they were slaves. At length two were caught
having full cargoes of slaves, and with these the
"Ione" returned to Zanzibar. Sayd had by this time
learned so much English, that, as Ned had hoped,
the office of interpreter was offered to him by
Commander Curtis. Sayd replied that he had
friends on shore whom he would consult on the
subject. The following day he returned.

"Are you going to remain with us?" asked Ned.

"After some time perhaps, not now," answered
Sayd, without giving any further reason for not
accepting the situation. He was as friendly as ever,
and expressed his gratitude for the kindness he had
received; he had, however, made up his mind to
remain on shore, and having bade farewell to Ned
and his other friends on board, he took his departure.

"I for one am glad to be rid of the fellow,"
observed Rhymer, as he was seated at the head of
the table in the midshipmen's berth. "Like all
Arabs, I have no doubt that he is a great rascal,
though he is so soft and insinuating in his manners."

"I hope that he is an exception to the rule,"
answered Ned, not liking to have his friend run
down.

"How dare you oppose your opinion to mine,

youngster?" exclaimed Rhymer. "As you claim the credit of saving his life, you think it necessary to praise him; but if any of us fall into his power, he'd show his gratitude by cutting our throats with as little compunction as any other Arab would have."

Charley sided with Ned; but the majority of those present thought Rhymer was not far wrong in the opinion he expressed.

The " Ione " having replenished her stores, again sailed on a cruise to the southward. Week after week, however, went by and not a prize was taken. It was very tantalising. Dhows were frequently seen and chased, but those which were overhauled proved to be legal traders. It was the old story over again. The Arabs were evidently too cunning to be caught; only those who had no cause to dread the British cruisers got in her way, and the rest kept out of it. That thousands of slaves were being embarked and carried northward there could be no doubt, but how to catch the dhows with slaves on board was the question. The commander resolved to try and outwit the Arabs. He had heard at Zanzibar that many of their vessels kept close in-shore, both to avoid the British cruisers and to fill up their cargoes with any negroes they might entrap. He accordingly determined to send the boats in with strong crews well armed and provisioned to lie in wait among the small islands off the shore, that should any dhows appear in sight, they might pounce down on them and effect their capture before they had time to make their escape. As the commander had no reason for keeping his plans secret they were soon known about the ship, and every one in the midshipmen's berth hoped to be employed in the service. Boat expeditions are always popular among men-of-war's men, notwithstanding the privations they entail, as a change from the regular routine of life on board ship. As yet it was not known who was to go; Ned and Charley thought that they should have but little chance.

"If we ask Mr. Hanson he will advise the commander to send us," said Ned.

"There's nothing like trying," replied Charley; "but I am afraid it will be of little use."

"I'll speak to him," said Ned. "It will show our zeal, and we can but be refused. I do not suppose that either you or I are likely to obtain command of a boat, but we may be sent with some one else, and the commander may be willing to give us an opportunity of gaining experience."

Ned carried out his intention.

"I will see about it," answered Mr. Hanson. "I suppose you and Meadows wish to go together to keep each other out of mischief."

"Thank you, sir," said Ned, "we'll look after each other at all events; it won't be our fault if we don't take a dhow or two."

"You are always zealous, Garth, and the commander will, I know, be glad to favour your wishes," answered the lieutenant, in a tone which encouraged Ned to hope that he would be sent on the expedition. While the ship was standing towards the African coast orders were received to prepare the three largest boats—the launch, pinnace, and cutter. The second lieutenant was to go in one with the assistant surgeon, the master in another, and Rhymer was to have charge of the third. The commander, who held him in more estimation than his messmates were wont to do, spoke to him on the quarter-deck.

"I intend to send two of the youngsters with you—Meadows and Garth. You will look after them, and see that they come to no harm; the experience they may gain will be of advantage to them."

"Of course, sir, I am always glad to be of service to youngsters, and will take good care of them," he answered aloud, muttering to himself, "especially as one of these days I may find them passed over my head."

"Very well, then, Rhymer, I will give you the necessary directions for your guidance; but remember you will on no account allow your men to sleep on shore on the mainland, and you must avoid remaining at night up any river into which you may chase a dhow."

Rhymer, of course, undertook to act according to the commander's directions.

Next day the ship came in sight of an island, three or four miles from the mainland, the western side rising some fifty or sixty feet above the summit of the water, and covered with trees. On the north side was a deep bay, into which the ship stood, and came to an anchor. Here she was hid both from the people on shore or from any passing dhows. The island formed one of a group, extending along the coast at various distances, most of them, however, were low, and many were mere sand-banks, with a few casuarina bushes growing on the higher portions. They would all, however, afford sufficient shelter to the boats, and conceal them till they could pounce out and capture any dhows passing near. The boats were now lowered, each with a gun in the bows, well stored with provisions and tents for living in on shore, while the crews were well armed, and were at once despatched to their several destinations. The second lieutenant was directed to go to the north-ward, and Rhymer was to proceed to the most southern limit, and in case of necessity they were to rendezvous at the spot from whence they started. The ship then sailed on a cruise to the northward, the commander promising to return in the course of a fortnight to replenish their provisions, and take charge of any dhows which might have been captured.

Ned and Charley were in high glee at the thoughts of the work they were to be engaged in. Old Rhymer had lately been more pleasant than usual, and they hoped to get along pretty well with him. He was fond of his ease, and in fine weather was likely to

entrust the boat to them, while he took a "caulk"
in the stern sheets ; indeed, when away from his
superiors, and in command himself, he was always
more amiable than on board ship.

For some time after the boat had shoved off all on
board were employed in re-stowing the stores, getting
her into trim, and placing the articles most likely to
be required uppermost. When everything had been
done according to his satisfaction, he addressed the
two midshipmen.

"Now, youngsters," he said, "recollect, I must
have implicit obedience, and all things will go well ;
if not, look out for squalls. I 'll take one watch, you,
Meadows, another, and you, Garth, the third."

The midshipmen made no answer, for, being as
well aware as he was of the importance of main-
taining discipline, they thought his remark rather
superfluous.

The weather continued fine, and the old mate
appeared to be in unusual good-humour. He laughed
and talked and spun long yarns which amused his
companions, although they had heard most of them
twenty times before. When tired of talking, he
stretched himself in the stern sheets to "take a
snooze," as he said, charging them to call him
should anything occur. " You see, youngsters, what
confidence I place in you," he observed. " I could
not venture to shut my eyes if I didn't feel sure that
you would keep a bright look-out. It is for your

good besides, that you may know how to act when left in command of a boat."

The midshipmen suspected that Rhymer thought more of his own comfort than of benefiting them. They passed several small islands. On some grew a scanty vegetation, while others were mere sand-banks. One of them was occupied by vast numbers of wild fowl, on which Rhymer looked with longing eyes.

"We might land, and in a short time kill birds enough to supply ourselves for a couple of days," he observed; " the delay cannot be of consequence."

Ned recollected that Rhymer had received orders to proceed without delay to the southward, but he knew that it would not do to remind him. The boat was therefore headed in towards a point on the lee side, where it appeared likely that an easy landing-place could be found. The beach, however, shelved so gradually that she could not approach within about twenty yards of the dry sand; she therefore was brought up by a grapnel, and Rhymer said that he would wade on shore, telling Ned to remain in charge of the boat with part of the crew, while Charley and the rest accompanied him. Neither Rhymer nor Charley had much experience as sportsmen, and as their arms were only ship's muskets, Ned thought it possible that they would not kill as many birds as Rhymer expected to obtain. Taking off their shoes and trousers, Rhymer and his followers jumped overboard and waded ashore.

There were but few birds on that end of the island, the chief colony being some way off. Ned heard several shots fired, but the sportsmen were too far off by that time for him to see whether any birds had been killed. In a short time the sounds of firing again reached him, evidently at a still greater distance; he did not forget his directions to keep a bright look-out, and he occasionally swarmed to the masthead that he might obtain a more extensive view. He had gone up for the fourth time, when he caught sight of a white sail coming up from the southward with the wind off the land; she was a dhow, of that there was no doubt, and might be a full slaver. She would possibly pass close to the island, abreast of which, as she was sailing rapidly, she would very quickly arrive. There was no time to be lost. He glanced his eye over the land, but could nowhere discover the shooting party; he was afraid of firing, for fear of alarming the crew of the dhow. As the only means of getting back Rhymer, he sent one of the men to try and find him and urge him to return. On came the dhow; every moment was precious; she had not yet discovered the boat. The man, wading on shore, ran off along the sand; the dhow was almost abreast of the island; at length Ned, to his relief, saw his companions approaching in the distance.

He got the sail ready, so that it might be hoisted the moment the party were on board. He shouted

and signed to them to make haste, pointing to the
dhow; at last Rhymer came, followed by Charley
and the men, wading through the water, puffing and
blowing, terribly out of wind. The result of the
sport appeared to be only half-a-dozen wild fowl, the
bodies of some being nearly blown to pieces. The
party quickly tumbled into the boat, and, the grapnel
being got up, she immediately made sail on a course
which Rhymer fancied would cut off the dhow. He
was evidently in no good-humour at the ill-success of
their sport, but the prospect of making a prize somewhat restored him; the dhow, however, must soon
have seen the boat standing out towards her.

"Hurrah! she knows it is no use running, and
gives in at once," exclaimed Rhymer, as the dhow
was seen to lower her canvas. He soon altered his
tone when she hoisted a much larger sail than she
had before been carrying, and put up her helm,
standing away directly before the wind.

"We must be after her, lads," cried Rhymer. "The
breeze may fail, and if she is becalmed we are sure to
have her."

It occurred to Ned that if Rhymer had not landed
on the island this would have been more likely.
The wind being light, the oars were got out and the
boat went along at a good rate.

"We shall have her, we shall have her!" cried the
old mate; "she is within range of our gun. Try a
shot, Meadows."

Charley sprang forward, and glancing along the piece, fired, but the shot fell short.

Though Rhymer still cried out, "We shall have her, we shall have her!" gradually his voice lost its tone of confidence, the breeze freshened, and the dhow began rapidly to distance her pursuer. Still the boat followed; the wind might again fail and the chase be overtaken. Instead of failing, however, the wind increased, and the dhow's hull sunk beneath the horizon. At length only the upper portion of her sail could be seen; still, as long as a speck was in sight, Rhymer pursued her, and not until the sun set did he abandon all hope.

"It is a bad job," he exclaimed. "Now let's have those birds, they must be pretty well stewed by this time."

The wild fowl had been cut up into pieces, and, with rice biscuits and other ingredients, had been stewing in the pot in which all their meals were cooked, officers and men sharing alike. As soon, however, as Rhymer's plate was handed to him he exclaimed—

"Fishy! Horribly fishy!"

"Strong flavoured I must own," said Charley; and he and Ned could with difficulty eat a small portion, though the men were not so particular. The unsavoury dish did not add to Rhymer's good-humour. Scarcely had supper been concluded than it began to blow so hard that it became necessary to take down two reefs,

and the boat close hauled stood towards the shore with
the prospect of having a dirty night of it. The sea, too,
got up and sent the spray flying over her. About the
middle watch rain began to fall heavily. Though
provided with an awning, blowing as fresh as it did, it
was impossible to rig it, and all hands were soon wet
through. As to sleeping, that was out of the question.
Rhymer passed the night grumbling and abusing the
wild fowl, the Arabs and the dhows, lamenting his own
hard fate in being engaged in such abominable service.
By morning, when the boat had got in again with the
land, the wind fell, and the sun rising, quickly dried
their wet clothes. After this heavy showers frequently
fell, detracting from the pleasure of the cruise. Ned
and Charley made themselves as happy as they could,
caring very little for Rhymer's grumbling. The worst
part of the business was that day after day went by and
no dhows were seen. Their destination, however, was
at length reached. It was an island with a snug little
harbour, in which the boat was perfectly concealed.
Here they were able to land and erect a tent, hidden
from the sea by a grove of casuarina bushes. A
couple of hands were kept on board the boat, while the
rest lived on shore and enjoyed the advantage of being
able to stretch their legs, but they were ordered to keep
within hail, in case of being required to shove off in
chase of a dhow. On the highest tree a look-out
place was made, reached by a rope ladder; and Rhymer
ordered Charley and Ned to occupy it by turns. Either

the one or the other had to sit, telescope in hand, from sunrise to sunset, sweeping the horizon in search of a sail. Several were seen, but they were too far off to make it of any use to go in chase. At length one appeared, which, by the course she was steering, would inevitably pass close to the island. Officers and crew hurried on board the boat, and away she pulled to cut off the stranger.

" We shall catch yonder craft this time, at all events," exclaimed Rhymer. " I only hope she will be full of slaves. As she stands on boldly, it is pretty clear that we are not seen."

The men gave way, in spite of the hot sun striking down on their heads. Still the dhow stood on, and in a short time the boat was up to her. A shot fired across her forefoot made the Arabs lower their sail, and the boat was pulled alongside. The crew jumped on board. About twenty fierce-looking Arabs stood on the deck, but they offered no resistance. Rhymer inquired for the captain. A well-dressed person stepped forward, making a profound salaam.

" Where are your papers ?" inquired Rhymer.

The Arab understood him, and presented several documents, which the English officer looked at, in as knowing a way as he could assume, without being able to decipher a word. He then made signs that he wished to examine the hold. No opposition was offered. It was found to contain a miscellaneous cargo, but not a single slave could be discovered.

As it was evident that the dhow was a lawful trader, Rhymer apologised to the captain, and stepping into his boat pulled for the shore, while the dhow sailed on her course. Several other dhows were boarded in the same way. Some had blacks on board, but they were supposed either to form part of the crew or to be passengers, and Rhymer did not venture to stop them. The time for their return was approaching.

"If we had not captured those slavers some time back, I should be inclined to believe that there is no such thing as the slave trade on this coast," exclaimed Rhymer, as he sat in the tent one evening after sunset. "It is all my ill-luck, however, and I suppose I shall get hauled over the coals for my want of success. If we catch sight of another dhow, and she takes to flight, I'll chase her round the world rather than lose her."

Next morning, soon after Ned had gone up to the look-out station, as he was turning his glass to the southward, the white canvas of a dhow, lighted up by the rays of the rising sun, came full into view, standing almost directly for the island. The wind for the last day or two had been variable. It was now blowing from the south-east. Quickly descending, he carried the information to his commanding officer. The party, tossing off their coffee, and snatching up the portions of breakfast they had just commenced, hurried on board. By the time they had got clear of the island the hull of the dhow could be seen. For some time she stood on as before, apparently not discovering them. With the wind as it had been, she had no chance of escaping, except by running on shore, and Rhymer ordered his men to lay on their oars to await her coming, while the sail was got ready to hoist in a moment, and the gun loaded to send a shot at her should she refuse to strike. Presently the wind shifted two points to the eastward, the dhow lowered her sail.

"Hurrah!" exclaimed Rhymer; "she knows it's of no use to try and escape. We will make sail, and shall soon be up to her. Hoist away!"

The boat was soon under canvas, heeling over to the freshening breeze. A short time, however, only had elapsed when the dhow was seen to rehoist her sail; but it was evident from her position that her head had been brought round, and was now pointing to the southward.

"It is pretty clear that the Arabs intend to run for it," observed Charley to Ned.

"And if they go round the world we shall have to follow them," answered Ned in a low voice.

The boat sailed well. There was just enough wind, and no more, to suit her, and the dhow apparently was not so fast a sailer as some of her class. Still she kept well ahead of the boat. Should the wind shift back to its old quarter, however, there was a fair probability that the boat would overtake her.

"We've got a good many hours of daylight, and

it will be a hard matter if we do not come up with her before dark," said Rhymer.

"But as it is, if we do not, and we are to chase her round the world, we must do our best to keep her in sight during the night," observed Charley, demurely.

The dhow was still out of range of the boat's gun, and appeared determined to stand on while there was a prospect of escaping. The wind continuing as before, Ned and Charley began to fear that after all she would get away.

"I wish that the breeze would shift back to the south-east, and we should have her sure enough, for we can sail three points closer to the wind than she can," observed Ned.

The time was passing by. Exciting as was the chase, the cook did not forget to prepare dinner, which the crew were as ready to eat as if no dhow supposed to be full of slaves was in sight. The evening approached, the compass showed that the dhow had fallen off two points, and presently afterwards another point.

"She 'll not weather that headland!" observed Charley, looking out ahead.

"No, but she's going to run on shore, and if so she'll go to pieces, and the slaves will either be drowned or be carried off into the interior," remarked Rhymer.

Presently the dhow was seen standing directly for

the coast. Ned, who was examining it through the telescope, exclaimed—

"There's the mouth of a river there, and she's steering for that."

"Then we'll follow her up it; if she can get in we can," answered Rhymer, and the boat's head was put towards the opening for which the dhow was making. Had there been a doubt on the subject before, there was now no longer any that the dhow was full of slaves, and that probably their captors would make every effort to retain them. As the boat drew nearer the entrance of the river, between two sandy points, it was difficult to judge whether or not it was a stream of any considerable size.

"If it's navigable for a hundred miles, we will follow the dhow up; I am not going to allow that craft to escape me," cried Rhymer.

The slaver was now running directly before the wind, fast distancing the boat, and was soon seen to enter the river, pitching and tossing as if she had crossed a bar. Rhymer steered on; two or three heavy rollers in succession lifted the boat, but no water broke on board, and she was soon safe in and gliding over the smooth surface of the stream. The river, which was of considerable width, was thickly lined on both sides by trees; in the middle of it the dhow was seen, running on with all her canvas set, still beyond reach of the boat's gun.

"We have her now, safe enough," exclaimed Rhymer;

"though, if the river is navigable far up from the mouth, she may lead us a long chase before we catch her."

"I only hope there may be no Arab fort up the river, or we may find it a difficult job to cut out the slaver after all," observed Charley.

"An Arab fort! What made you think of that, youngster?" exclaimed Rhymer, looking somewhat blank. "If there is we shall have more fighting than we bargained for, but it will never do to go back without attempting to secure the dhow."

"I should think not," remarked Ned.

The men of course were ready for any work their officers determined on. The excitement of the chase and the prospect of fighting before them was greatly increased as the dhow got higher up the river; the wind falling, and sometimes becoming baffling, the boat gained on her. Ned was sent forward to look out for the fort, but he could discover no signs of a stockade; at any moment, however, a bend of the stream might disclose it to view.

"Get out the oars!" cried Rhymer; "before long I hope the wind will fail the dhow altogether and we shall soon be up to her."

The men gave way, in a few minutes the boat got the dhow within range of her gun.

"We must try to bring her sail down," exclaimed Rhymer, giving the helm to Charley and springing forward to the gun. He fired, the shot went through the sail, but the chase stood on as before; the gun was quickly loaded, but the second shot, though well aimed, produced no more result than the first. It was pretty evident that the Arabs expected to reach some place of shelter, and that they would run on until they had gained it. This made Rhymer doubly anxious to come up with them before they could do so. He continued firing away as fast as the gun could be run in and loaded. Though the sail was riddled with shot, the yard and rigging remained uninjured.

" Get the muskets ready, Garth ! " he cried out. "We shall soon be near enough to send a shower of bullets among those fellows, and they will then, I have a notion, heave to pretty quickly."

Scarcely, however, had he spoken than the breeze freshened up, and to his disappointment he found that the boat was no longer gaining on the dhow. Still he kept firing the gun, hoping that a fortunate shot might bring down her yard. Some way ahead, on the south side of the river, he observed a small bay, where the bank was steeper than in any other place and free of trees; the dhow appeared to be edging away towards it. "I must knock away that fellow's yard. I'd give a hundred guineas to see it come down," he exclaimed, as he again fired.

The shot wounded the yard, for he could see the splinters fly from it, but it still remained standing; at any moment, however, it might go. The Arabs seemed to think so likewise, for the dhow was now steered directly for the little bay. Before another shot was fired at her, she was close up to the bank, and a black stream of human beings was seen issuing forth from her decks, and winding, like a long black snake, up among the grass and bushes, while the Arabs could be distinguished by their dress urging on the fugitives with their spears.

"We must stop those fellows, and turn them back," exclaimed Rhymer, and resuming the tiller, he steered the boat for the shore at the nearest spot above the dhow where a landing could be effected.

"Meadows, do you remain by the boat with a couple of hands, the rest of you follow me," he exclaimed as he leapt on shore.

It was now seen that the blacks, of whom there appeared to be nearly two hundred, were becoming divided, some going off in one direction, some in another, while others, mostly women and children, were sinking down on the ground, unable to keep up with their companions. Rhymer on this made chase with most of his crew after the larger party ; but he had not got far when he ordered Ned, with the cockswain, Dick Morgan by name, and two other hands, to pursue another who were going off to the left.

Ned, as directed, started away at full speed, and soon outstripped his followers, who, as they overtook smaller parties of the blacks, tried to turn them back. The negroes on hearing the shouts of the sailors, and seeing them flourish their cutlasses, more frightened than ever, sank down to the ground. In vain the seamen endeavoured to make them rise, assuring them that they meant them no harm. Much time was lost in the attempt. Ned, in obedience to his orders, had got ahead of one party of the blacks and was seen by Dick Morgan making signs to induce them to stop running. When, however, Dick looked again, he could nowhere discover his young officer, while the slaves were scampering off at a rate which made it almost hopeless to overtake them.

"Lads, we must not let Mr. Garth be carried off by those niggers, for it seems to me that they have somehow or other got hold of him," exclaimed Dick, shouting to his companions.

Away they dashed after the fugitives. They had got some distance when they heard Mr. Rhymer hailing them to come back. Dick pointed in the direction where he had last seen the midshipman ; but Mr. Rhymer not understanding his signs, peremptorily ordered him and his companions to retreat to the boat. It was time indeed to do so, for a large party of well armed Arabs appeared on the hill just before them, and with threatening gestures were advancing evidently with the intention of recovering the slaves they had captured. Rhymer saw at once that were he to remain he should run the risk of having his whole party cut off, and that his only safe course was to retreat as fast as possible to the boat; he accordingly gave the word to face about, and by threatening to fire, he kept the Arabs in check. Their object was evidently not so much to attack the English, as to get possession of the slaver. Had the boat been nearer the dhow, Rhymer might have boarded her and set her on fire, but in endeavouring to do so, he might expose his whole party to destruction. Had there been time even to get hold of any of the blacks, they could not have been taken into the boat, and Rhymer had therefore to make the best of his way down to her without securing a single one of them. The Arabs, who advanced more rapidly as they saw the English retreating, soon got under shelter of some trees, whence they opened a hot fire from matchlocks and gingalls. Rhymer ordered his men to fire in return, but their exposed position on the bank of the river, and their inferior numbers, rendered the combat unequal.

Rhymer, who was as brave as most men, at first hoped to drive the enemy from their shelter, but he soon saw that he might lose many of his.men in the attempt, and that his only prudent course was to get on board and shove off as fast as possible. Three of his men had already been hit; should he remain longer the crew might be so weakened as to be unable to pull the boat down the river. Charley, who had run the boat in ready to receive them when he saw them coming, was dismayed at not discovering Ned among the party.

" Where is Mr. Garth ?" he exclaimed. "Have none of you seen him ?"

Rhymer repeated the question.

Dick Morgan was the only man who could answer it : he replied that he had last set eyes on him while trying to induce the blacks to return to the dhow.

" Have they killed him, do you think ?" asked Charley, in a tone which showed his anxiety.

" Can't say, sir ; but if not, it is more than likely that those Arab fellows have got hold of him, and I 'm afraid they 'll not be treating him over well."

Just then, however, there was no time to make further inquiries. The first thing to be done was to get out of reach of the Arabs' matchlocks.

Rhymer gave the word to shove off, and the boat pulled away from the bank. He was vexed at the utter failure of the enterprise, and the blame which might be attributed to him for the loss of Ned. He might still, however, destroy the dhow. The Arabs, well aware of the long range of the boat's gun, were still keeping at a distance. There would be time to get up to the dhow and to set her on fire. Rhymer accordingly steered in where she lay, with the boat's gun ready to send a shot into the midst of any party who might venture to show themselves. Almost before the Arabs were aware of what was intended, the boat was up to the dhow, matches had been got ready, and the seamen springing on board, in less than a minute had set her on fire fore and aft. The combustible materials with which she was fitted quickly blazed up, and her destruction was inevitable. The men leapt back into the boat, which now pulled away out of gun-shot into the middle of the stream.

" Surely we are not to leave Garth without going to look for him!" exclaimed Charley. " Perhaps he may be hiding himself somewhere, and will, when the Arabs retire, make his way down to the margin of the river expecting to be taken off."

" Very little chance of that; but, depend on it, I 'll not show my face on board without him if I can help it," answered Rhymer.

Charley was obliged to be content with this promise. As he watched the shore through his telescope he could see the Arabs collecting the unfortunate slaves and driving them on before them, though he in vain searched for Ned among the former. Had he been made a prisoner he would probably have been seen. This made him hope that he might still be recovered. At length Rhymer began to grow impatient. The last of the slaves had been carried off, and the Arabs themselves had disappeared behind the hill. Charley now entreated Rhymer to pull in for the shore. " If you will let me I will land with any of the men who will volunteer, and we will search round in every direction for Garth ; he may possibly have been wounded, and have crawled under some bushes to hide himself from the Arabs."

Rhymer hesitated. " If I let you go you may be

caught also, and I shall have to report the loss of two midshipmen instead of one."

" O no, no! Do let me go!" cried Charley, in a beseeching tone. " The Arabs have gone away, and we will keep a good look-out not to be suprised. I am sure that some of the men will be ready to go with me."

" I will!" exclaimed Dick Morgan.

" And I, and I, and I," added others, until the whole boat's crew volunteered.

At last Rhymer, feeling that he might be accused of deserting the midshipman, consented, allowing Morgan with three other men to accompany Charley.

The boat accordingly returned to the shore. While Charley and his men pushed forward, Rhymer and the remainder having landed, advanced a short distance to support him in case he should have to retreat. Charley led the way to a spot pointed out by Morgan, where Ned had last been seen. They hunted about among the bushes, but no trace of him could they discover.

" Ned Garth, Ned Garth! where are you?" shouted Charley again and again, forgetting in his anxiety that the Arabs might hear, but no answer reached him. There were, however, traces of the course the blacks had taken, wherever the ground was soft enough to receive impressions of their feet. Charley was tempted to follow, and the men, regardless of consequences, accompanied him. He had not gone far when he came upon two children who had evidently been let fall by those who were carrying them. Both were dead, and their shrunken little forms showed that they had died from starvation. The top of the hill was reached. Charley at length stopped and looked round, but neither Arabs nor blacks were anywhere visible. Though, had he consulted his own feelings, he would have gone on still farther, he remembered his promise to be cautious, and exclaimed with a heavy heart—

" We must go back ; we may still find him, but I dare not push on further."

The men appeared to share his feelings, for Ned was a favourite with all of them. They made their way towards the boat, searching the bushes as they went along, dreading tha at any moment they might discover Ned's body. At length they met Rhymer.

" He must have been made prisoner and carried off by the Arabs," cried Charley ; " that is the only consolation we have."

" Well, I suppose they would scarcely have taken the trouble to carry him off if he had been killed ; and we must report to the commander that such is the conclusion we have arrived at, after making diligent search for him in all directions."

Charley felt somewhat indignant that Rhymer did not express more regret at the loss of their young messmate ; he, however, said nothing. They once more embarked, and shoving off, proceeded down the river. It was important to get over the bar before dark, and make the best of their way back to the

ship, for the wounded men, now that the **excitement**
was over, began to complain of their hurts, and it
was, of course, necessary that they should be attended
to by the surgeon with as little delay as possible.
As the wind blew almost up the river, it was necessary
to get the oars out and pull the boat over the bar.
This was a heavy task with a diminished crew, but
Rhymer sent one of the wounded men to the helm,
while he took one oar and Charley another.

They got down very well to the mouth, but the
heavy foam-topped rollers which came tumbling in
threatened to prevent them getting into the open sea
beyond.

"It must be done," exclaimed Rhymer. "To-
morrow it may be worse, and we shall have a whole
fleet of Arab boats coming down upon us."

Twice, however, he pulled up to the inner roller,
and backed the boat off again. For some minutes he
stood up watching the seas ; at length he exclaimed,
"Now, my lads, now or never, give way," and all
hands bending their backs to the oars, pulled on as
British seamen are wont to do in cases of emergency.
It was a struggle truly for life and death. Had the
boat been caught broadside by one of those treacherous
undulations, she would have been thrown over and
over, and not a man on board could have escaped.
Had an oar broken, or the men relaxed in their
efforts, no power could have saved them. Three
rollers had been passed, there were still two more to

be encountered. The fourth advanced with a crest of foam. The boat had almost reached the summit, when the water came rushing over her bows, half-filling her; but the crew persevered, and the wounded men began bailing away with might and main.

"Pull away, pull away, lads!" shouted Rhymer; "there's only one more, and we shall be clear of them."

Again the boat rose, the water rushing aft, but the poor fellows seated there, in spite of their hurts, continued to heave it out. The next minute, having forced their way over the last roller, the boat was free. They had still a long pull before them until the boat could obtain a good offing, so that they might make sail and stand to the northward. At length the sails were set. By this time it was perfectly dark, yet, having a compass, a proper course could be kept. As the wind was light, it was not until near morning that they reached the island where they had left their tent and stores. As there was a moon they were able to steer into the bay. On landing they hurried up to where the tent had stood.

" Why, where is it ?" exclaimed Rhymer.

They hunted about, neither their tent nor any of their stores could they discover.

" Some fellows have been here and carried them off, no doubt about that," observed Charley; " but who they are is more than I can say."

"The rascally crew of a dhow probably," answered Rhymer. "How the villains must have laughed at us when they saw our boat sailing away."

A further search in no way cleared up the mystery, and all they could do was to light a fire and cook some provisions, which had fortunately been kept on board the boat. On the return of daylight they found the marks of numerous naked feet on the sand ; but whether of blacks or Arabs they were unable to determine, though Charley suspected that they were those of a party of blacks who had come across from the mainland.

This loss made it still more important for them to get back to the ship. As soon as they had taken a hurried breakfast, Rhymer ordered all hands on board, and once more they made sail to the northward.

The old mate, as may be supposed, was in an especial ill-humour, which he vented on poor Charley, who required comforting for the loss of his friend. For three days he had to endure all the abuse heaped on him, but he bore it without complaint, resolving not again, if he could help it, to take a long cruise with Rhymer. At length a sail was seen ahead, standing towards them. As she drew nearer—

"That's her, that's the old ship!" cried Morgan, who was on the look-out.

Dick was right, and in another hour the ship hove to and the boat got alongside. Rhymer's downcast countenance showed that he had unsatisfactory intelligence to communicate. The commander listened to his report, but made no remark; he then desired to hear Charley's account.

"We can't let the poor boy be lost without a further effort to recover him!" observed Captain Curtis.

He sent for Mr. Hanson, and they held a consultation. The result was that the commander determined, having already picked up the other boats, to proceed to the mouth of the river and to send them in to inquire from the first Arabs they could meet with what had become of the missing midshipman and to insist on his liberation.

There was a chance also of their capturing a dhow laden with the slaves which had been landed. The ship came off the mouth of the river at night, and the boats were got ready to go in over the bar as soon as there was light sufficient to see their way, by which time also the flood would have made. Mr. Hanson begged to have charge of the expedition, as he felt an especial interest in the recovery of Ned. The boats pulled up at a rapid rate, and soon reached the spot where the encounter had taken place. Charley, who had accompanied Mr. Hanson, kept a look-out along the bank, half expecting to see a signal made by Ned. No one appeared, and if there were any inhabitants, they kept out of sight. The boats pulled up the river for ten miles or more, till

Mr. Hanson's, which was leading, grounded. **No** trace of the missing midshipman was discovered, and, much disappointed, the expedition returned to the ship.

The weather proving fine, the "Ione" remained at anchor. Every day a boat was sent in ready to receive the midshipman should he appear, but returned with the same unsatisfactory report.

The commander, considering that everything possible had been done to recover the midshipman, then ordered the ship to be got under weigh, and she stood for Zanzibar, where he hoped, by other means, to be more successful, although the general opinion on board was that poor Garth had been killed, and that nothing more would be heard of him.

CHAPTER VIII.

THE "Ione" had been upwards of three years on the station, and of late the sick list had been greatly increased, still the commander persevered in his efforts to capture slavers; but the Arabs, grown cautious, managed to avoid him, and for some time not a single dhow had been taken.

One morning, as the ship lay becalmed on the shining ocean, with the sun's rays beaming down as from a furnace on the heads of the crew, the smoke of a steamer was seen coming from the southward. She rapidly approached, and coming nearer, made her number. She was a man-of-war. Had she came out to relieve the "Ione"? Every eye on board watched her eagerly. Stopping her way a boat was lowered; her commander came on board. No sooner were the contents of the despatch he brought known than cheers rose from fore and aft, joined in by the poor fellows in their hammocks. The "Ione" was to return home immediately. Before long a breeze sprang up, the two ships parted, and the corvette, under all sail, steered for the Cape.

"The only thing I regret is going home without nearing of young Garth," observed the commander, as he walked the deck with his first lieutenant; "I would have given much to find him, but I fear that when he fell into their hands, the rascally Arabs killed him."

"I am inclined to your notion, sir," answered Mr. Hanson; "but I still have a lingering hope that by some means or other he may have escaped, although, as, notwithstanding all our inquiries and the rewards offered, no tidings of him had reached Zanzibar when we left the island, it is, I confess, very faint indeed."

Charley Meadows was the only person in the midshipmen's berth who would not abandon all expectation of again seeing his friend, and who would very gladly have remained another year on the station with the chance of hearing of Ned. He dreaded also the melancholy duty which might fall to his lot of informing Lieutenant Pack and Miss Sarah and sweet Mary of Ned's fate.

As the ship drew near England he thought over and over again of what he should say; no one had written, as the commander had been unwilling to alarm the boy's friends while any uncertainty existed. They would, therefore, on seeing the announcement in the papers of the "Ione's" return, be looking out eagerly for him. The corvette had a rapid passage, and on reaching Portsmouth was at once paid off. Charley Meadows had written to his father, who was still commander of the coast-guard station at Long-view, giving an account of what had occurred, and begging him to break the intelligence to Lieutenant Pack. As soon as he was at liberty he hurried home. One of the first questions he put on his arrival was, "Have you told them, father, about poor Ned?"

"No; for I only received your letter yesterday, and have been unable to get over and see our friends. It will be sad news to them. Whenever I have called on Pack and his sister, their nephew was always the subject of their conversation."

Charley thus found that, after all, he must be the first to carry the sad intelligence to his friends. He, however, possessed the most valuable description of courage; he was morally, as well as physically, brave. The duty had to be performed, and he resolved to do it forthwith. As his father could not go, he set out by himself. Now and then he stopped to consider what he should say, and then hurried on, wishing to say it at once. Just before he reached Triton Cottage, he saw Mr. Pack coming along the road; the old lieutenant stopped and looked at Charley as he approached, putting out his hand.

"Glad to welcome you, my lad. I saw that the 'Ione' had arrived and was to be paid off, so was looking out for you; but where is Ned? I thought you would have come down together."

Now came the moment Charley had dreaded.

"I will tell you how it happened,. sir, directly ; but Ned is not with us. I don't believe he is lost, and no one saw him dead; but the Arabs got hold of him, and he has not since turned up."

"What! hasn't he come home with you?" exclaimed the lieutenant. "You don't mean to say that our Ned is dead?"

"No, sir; but he's lost, and we don't know what has become of him," and Charley then gave a full account of all that had occurred.

The old lieutenant listened attentively. "Poor Sally! poor Mary!" he murmured, as, leaning on Charley's shoulder, he walked back to the house. "It will well-nigh break their hearts to hear that he is dead, but I for one won't believe it; I tell you, Meadows, I can't believe it," his voice growing more husky as he spoke. "I expect to see Ned a commander before I die; he is sure to get on in the service. Sally won't believe it either; she's got too much good sense for that. Come along, however, you shall tell her and Mary about it, for I have not taken in all the particulars."

The lieutenant stumped on, but Charley felt the hand which rested on his shoulder press more and more heavily. They together entered the parlour, where Miss Sarah and Mary were seated.

"Ned, Ned!" cried Miss Sally, mistaking him for her nephew; but she quickly saw her mistake, while Mary knew him at once.

"Where is Ned?" they both inquired, after they had shaken hands, Mary looking up into his face with an inquiring glance.

"He hasn't come home with us," said Charley, "and Mr. Pack will tell you what I have told him."

The lieutenant was glad of this opportunity to give his own version of the story, for he was afraid Charley would alarm his sister and Mary.

"You see Ned's not come home in the 'Ione,' and that's a disappointment, I'll own. That he is all right I have no doubt, somewhere out in Africa among some Arabs who got hold of him while performing his duty—you may be sure Ned would be always doing that—and he hasn't yet been able to make his way down to the coast, or at all events to get on board an English ship. He'll do so by-and-by though. You two must not fret about him in the meantime. I know what Ned's made of; he has a fine constitution, and is not likely to succumb to the climate; and as to the Arabs, except in the matter of slavery, they are not a bad set of fellows."

Thus the lieutenant ran on, until Miss Sarah, turning to Charley, asked him to give a more particular account. This he did, omitting no circumstance which might support the idea that Ned had escaped.

Miss Sarah every now and then interrupted him with an ejaculation or a question, but poor Mary sat looking very pale and anxious, with her eyes fixed upon his countenance all the time and not uttering a word.   Tom Baraka had seen Charley arrive with the lieutenant, and guessing that he had belonged to the "Ione," and had brought news of Ned, waited outside, hoping to learn from him why Ned had not come home.   At length, however, unable to endure the suspense, he took the privilege of a favoured servant and came into the room.

"You come from de 'Ione,' massa?" he said, looking at Charley. "Pray tell me why Massa Ned not come back.   Hab him gone in nudder ship?"

Charley, who remembered Tom, briefly told him the particulars of Ned's disappearance.

"Den I go an' look for him!" exclaimed Tom. "He go search for my boy, what I do better dan go look for him?"

"O do, do!" cried Mary, springing up. "I would go too if I could be of any use."

"You do not know the character of the country, Miss Mary," said Charley; "but if Tom would go, if he escapes being caught by the Arabs, he would have a better chance of finding him than any one else. How to get there would be the difficulty, unless he could obtain a passage on board a man-of-war going out to the coast."

"Yes, yes, I go!" cried Tom; "I find a way, nebber fear."

"We must think the matter over, and consider what can be done," said the lieutenant. "Ask your father, Charley, to come here and give me the benefit of his advice, and I will write to Hanson, they'll have his address at the Admiralty, and he will come down here and tell us what he thinks best, or I'll go up to London myself and see their lordships. They would not wish a promising young officer to be lost without taking all possible steps for his recovery."

Charley's spirits rose as he found his friends even more sanguine than himself as to the finding of Ned. They talked on and on without any material alteration in their proposed plan. The lieutenant said that he would write to Mr. Farrance, as in duty bound, to tell him of Ned's disappearance, and to ask his advice. "He has the means of helping us, and judging from the generous way in which he has acted towards Ned, I feel sure that we can rely on him," he observed.

Charley went back with a message to his father, who came over that evening, and the subject was again discussed in all its bearings, indeed the old lieutenant could think and talk of nothing else. He had, in the meantime, despatched his letters to Mr. Farrance and the late first lieutenant of the "Ione," and determined, by the advice of Mr. Meadows, to take no steps until he heard from them.

The next day Charley again came over, and greatly interested Mary and her aunt by the account he gave of their adventures in the Indian Ocean. He inspired Mary with a strong wish to see the horrible traffic in slaves put an end to.

"If I had a fortune I would devote it to that object," she exclaimed enthusiastically. "What sufferings the poor little children have to endure; and then the agony of their parents as they are dragged off from their homes to die on their way to the sea, or on board those horrible dhows, or to be carried into slavery, which must be worse than death."

Her remarks had greater influence on Charley than even the miserable state of the slaves on board the dhows had produced. "I will do all I can to try and get back to the coast as soon as possible, or if an expedition is formed to go up the country to look for Ned I'll get my father to allow me to join it; I am pretty well seasoned to the climate by this time— never had an hour's illness while I was away."

By return of post a letter was received from Mr. Farrance. He sympathised with the lieutenant and his sister in their anxiety about their nephew; said that he would be glad to defray the expenses should any plan be formed for discovering him, and begged to see Mr. Pack in town as soon as possible.

The old lieutenant accordingly at once made preparations for his journey. Fortunately, before he started, he received a letter from Mr. Hanson, saying that in the course of three or four days he would come down.

"I shall be in time to stop him," observed the lieutenant, "and to talk the matter over with him before I see Mr. Farrance, who will, of course, want all the information I can give him. I'll take Tom with me; he knows his own country, and his woolly pate contains as much good sense as many a white man's skull."

Tom could scarcely restrain the delight he felt on hearing of his master's decision.

"But who take care ob de house, de pigs, and de garden, and de poultry?" he exclaimed of a sudden, as if the idea had just struck him.

"The ladies and Jane will attend to them, and no one will think of robbing the house during our absence," was the answer.

The lieutenant and his black attendant set off the following morning and reached London in safety, arriving just in time to stop Mr. Hanson from going down to Triton Cottage.

He doubted whether the Admiralty would consider themselves justified in sending out any special expedition, and they had already given directions to the vessels on the coast to make all inquiries in their power, but he thought that a private expedition such as his friend suggested might possibly succeed, although he was not very sanguine on the subject. Young Garth might possibly be alive, and until they had received proof positive of his death hope ought not to be abandoned. He was expecting his own promotion, but should he not obtain it, he should be ready to go out in command of a properly organised expedition. Trustworthy natives might be found, they were not all so black as generally described. A private vessel, which would remain on the coast while the expedition pushed inland, would entail considerable cost. Where were the funds to come from ?

When the old lieutenant related Mr. Farrance's offer to defray all expenses, his friend's countenance brightened.

"That alters the case; we will see him without delay, and if he has the means we are right to take advantage of his liberality," said Mr. Hanson.

The two officers, therefore, accompanied by Tom Baraka, proceeded to the address of Mr. Farrance in one of the fashionable parts of London. The old lieutenant was somewhat taken aback, as he expressed it, on finding himself in a handsome mansion, such as he had never before in his life entered; it appeared to him a perfect palace. He and his companion were at once ushered into a large study, where they found Mr. Farrance, who, rising from his seat, welcomed them cordially. He expressed his sincere regret at hearing of the disappearance of his young friend, from whose commander, he said, he had received excellent accounts. "We must find him if he is to be found. What object the Arabs can have for keeping him in captivity, when a reward has been offered for his liberation, it is difficult to say. However, I am very glad to have the means of assisting to recover him."

Mr. Farrance, after putting numerous questions to the two officers and Tom, observed, " We will consider the matter settled. I have two objects in view; besides the recovery of our young friend, I am sure the more the natives are brought into intercourse with white men who show that they come for the purpose of benefiting them, the sooner will the slave trade be put a stop to and the Arabs driven out of the country. Not until then will the negroes be able to enjoy the blessings of peace, and the possibility of advancing in civilisation and embracing the truths of Christianity. As you, Lieutenant Pack, know those seas and are willing to take charge of a vessel, I shall be glad to obtain for you the command of one suited for the purpose; and I conclude, as you would find it inconvenient to travel—indeed you should not make the attempt—you would remain on board while the rest of the party penetrate into the interior. You, I dare say, Mr. Hanson, can get some trustworthy men among your late crew to accompany you; but we must rely chiefly on the natives for furnishing a sufficient force."

Mr. Hanson was delighted with the readiness shown by Mr. Farrance to forward their object, and

he and his brother officer at once promised to under
take the arrangement of an expedition.

"No time then must be lost," replied Mr. Farrance. "I give you and Lieutenant Pack authority
to obtain such a vessel as you consider fit for the
purpose, and to engage a crew for her, and companions for your land journey. You will, I conclude,
select a small craft which can keep close in with the
coast or run up rivers, as every mile you can go by
water will save you so much, or probably a still
greater distance of land journey."

Further arrangements having been made, the two
officers and Tom Baraka took their departure, promising to report progress.

Mr. Hanson was not a man to let the grass grow
under his feet, and the old lieutenant was even more
eager than his friend to get under weigh.

Within three days they paid another visit to Mr.
Farrance. They had purchased a schooner of about
150 tons, which had once been a yacht—a fast craft.
Hands had been engaged, chiefly from the crew of the
"Ione"; three men from Cowes accustomed to fore and
aft vessels, one of whom was to act as mate. The
fitting out of the schooner would be an easy matter,
but the preparations for the land journey required
more time and consideration. The only two people
who had as yet undertaken to go were Charley
Meadows and Tom Baraka. Two stout Africans who
had lately arrived in England on board a ship from

India, and who stated that when boys they had been captured on the east coast, but had escaped from Madagascar, to which island they had been carried, to an English merchantman, appeared well suited for the undertaking. Mr. Hanson was only waiting until he could hear more about them.

Being satisfied with their testimonials he engaged them, and the next day, as he was prosecuting his search in the neighbourhood of the docks, he met with an Arab and three Lascars, of whom, on inquiry of the masters of the ships who brought them home, he obtained a favourable report. The Lascars were brave and useful fellows, while the Arab spoke English fairly, and he had already penetrated some way into the interior of Africa.

Both officers, assisted by Charley Meadows, who had been sent for, were engaged from morning until night in superintending the preparations. The old lieutenant when he quitted home had expected to return, but as the "Hope" was ready for sea, he changed his purpose and wrote to his sister explaining his reasons.

"I don't want to go through another parting, Sally," he said. "You know I love you and Mary with all my heart, but that heart is not so tough as it ought to be perhaps, and I could not bear saying 'good-bye' again, when I have said it already, although I didn't think it was for long. If Ned is found, and I make no doubt about the matter, we shall have, I pray God, a happy meeting, and I expect to find Mary grown at least an inch taller, tell her. Don't either of you fret; whatever happens all will be for the best—of that you may be sure. Should it please Him who governs all things to call me away— and I do not shut my eyes to the possibility—you will find my will in my desk. I have provided, as far as I can, for you and Mary."

This letter was received the very morning the " Hope " was to sail. It caused considerable disappointment to Aunt Sally and Mary, but they could not help confessing that after all it was for the best.

" My good brother always acts wisely," said Aunt Sally. " It would have cost us a good deal to say ' good-bye,' when we knew he was going away to that terrible country Africa ! "

" Pernaps the ' Hope ' will come off here," observed Mary ; " we shall then see uncle and Tom Baraka, and perhaps Mr. Hanson and Charley, and be able to send messages by them to Ned. As they sailed this morning, they may be off here in a couple of days."

Mary, as may be supposed, kept a constant lookout through the lieutenant's telescope, but time went by and no schooner appeared. Some days afterwards a letter, which had been landed by a pilot vessel, brought information that the " Hope " was already in the chops of the channel and all well. Aunt Sally and Mary at first felt a great blank in their existence. The lieutenant's cheery voice was no longer heard, and his chair stood vacant at their daily meals, while, instead of the master, Miss Sally led the morning and evening prayer to the diminished household. Tom Baraka's merry laugh was also missed, for in spite of his one absorbing thought, he was merry when ho gave way to his natural disposition.

Aunt Sally and Mary did not, however, neglect their usual avocations. They had plenty of work now that Jane had not time to assist them.

The garden had to be attended to, and they persevered in their visits to the neighbouring poor. Mary very frequently went to see Mr. Shank. The old man received her with more apparent gratitude than he used before to exhibit, and willingly listened when she read to him. He was evidently deeply interested in the account she gave him of the expedition in search of Ned, as also when she repeated the information she had received from Charley Meadows about Africa and the slave trade.

" Terrible, terrible," he muttered, " that men should sell each other for gold and produce all this suffering, and yet——" he was silent and seemed lost in thought. Mary did not for some minutes again speak. She then continued—

" It is the duty of all who have the means to try and put a stop to this fearful state of things, and to assist in sending missionaries of the Gospel and artisans to teach Christianity to the poor blacks, and to instruct them in the useful arts of civilised life."

"The Government should do that," said Mr. Shank. "We pay them taxes."

"The Government do their part by sending out ships-of-war to stop the dhows and the Arabs who steal the slaves, making the trade so difficult and dangerous a one that many will be compelled to give it up—so uncle says—and what more than that can the Government do ? Private people must carry on the rest of the work, and a more noble and glorious one I am sure cannot be found. If I had ever so much money, I should like to spend it in that way."

"But you would get no interest, you would see no result," said the old man.

Mary pointed to the Bible she had brought, and from which she had previously been reading. "There is a verse there which tells us that we are to lay up riches in heaven, where neither moth nor rust doth corrupt, and where thieves do not break through and steal," she answered in an unaffected tone. "I should not expect interest, and I am very sure that I should be satisfied with the result."

The old man again mused, this time far longer than before. "And so you want to make Christians and civilised men of those black Africans of whom you spoke ? " he observed.

"Yes ; it is the only way to make them become happy here and happy hereafter," she said, energetically. "I am sure of it. If all the money that is hoarded up or spent uselessly were devoted to such a work, how soon might the condition of the unfortunate negroes be changed for the better."

"Then do you blame those who hoard up money?" asked the old man.

"Yes, indeed I do. I think they are wicked, very wicked, and are not making a good use of the talents committed to them. They are just as wicked as those who throw it away or spend it badly."

"You are a severe censor, Miss Mary," said the old man. "But you are right, very right." He placed his hand on his brow.

Mary took her leave, feeling more drawn towards Mr. Shank than she had ever before been, he seemed so softened and so sad, and very much weaker than he had before appeared.

Mary told her aunt.

"He suffers from want of food," observed Miss Sally. "You shall go again to-morrow and take him another pudding, and say that I will send one for him, if he wishes it, every day."

Mary reached Mr. Shank's door. She heard him feebly approaching to withdraw the bolts; as soon as he had done so, he tottered back, panting, to his seat.

"I am glad you have come, Mary, or I might have been found stiff and cold on my bed. I am very ill, I fear, for I have never felt before as I do now," he said, in so low and trembling a voice that Mary had to draw closer to hear him.

She begged him to eat the food she had brought,

hoping that it might restore his strength. He followed her advice, lifting the spoon slowly to his mouth.

After he had finished the food he appeared somewhat stronger.

"Thank you, Mary," he said. "I owe you a great deal more than I can now tell you, for I have something else to say. I want you to bring me a lawyer, an honest man, if such is to be found, and his clerk must come to witness my signature. I'll try to keep alive until he arrives, for, Mary, do you know I think that I am dying."

"O no, I hope not, Mr. Shank. You are only weak from want of food," exclaimed Mary, who, however, was much alarmed. "I will go on to where Mr. Thorpe lives, I know the way perfectly, and have heard uncle say that he is a good and honest man, and is trusted by all the people round."

"Go then, Mary, go !" said the old man. "Don't allow any one to stop you ; and if Mr. Thorpe is out, write a message requesting him to come on here immediately."

Mary, promising Mr. Shank that she would obey his wishes, hastened away. She observed that he did not close the door behind her as usual. She found Mr. Thorpe at home and gave her message.

"What! old Shank the miser ? I suspect that he has something worth leaving behind," observed the lawyer. "I'll be with him immediately, depend on

that. But how are you going to get back, young
lady ? "

" Oh, I can walk perfectly well," said Mary.

" No; let me drive you as far as old Shank's, and
if you like to remain I will take you on to Triton
Cottage. Miss Sally will not know what has become
of you."

Mary was glad to accept this offer, and the lawyer's
gig being brought round, she took her seat between
him and his clerk.

" I will wait outside," she said when they reached
Mr. Shank's door. "I can look after your horse and
see it doesn't run away, for Mr. Shank may have
something particular to tell you which he might not
wish me to hear."

The lawyer, appreciating Mary's delicacy, agreed,
though he did not give her the charge of his horse,
as the animal was well accustomed to stand with its
head fastened to a paling while he visited his clients.

Mary waited and waited, sometimes walking about,
at others standing beside the gig, or sitting on the hill-
side, on the very spot which had often been occupied
by Ned. Her thoughts naturally flew away to him.
Where could he be all this time ? Would Mr. Hanson and Charley discover him, or would they return
without tidings of his fate ?

The lawyer at last appeared, and, directing his
clerk to return home with some papers he held in his
hand, he begged Mary to get into the gig.

"I must run in to see old Mr. Shank first," she
said, "and learn if there is anything aunt or I can do
for him."

"You will find him more easy in his mind than he
was when I arrived; but in regard to assistance, he
doesn't require it as much as you suppose. He has
consented to let me send a doctor, and a respectable
woman to attend on him. He is not in a fit state to
be left by himself."

Mary was surprised at these remarks. Not wishing
to delay the lawyer she hurried in. Mr. Shank, who
was still seated in his arm-chair, put out his shrivelled
hand and clasped hers.

"Thank you, Mary, thank you!" he said. "You
deserve to be happy, and Heaven will bless your kindness to a forlorn old man. I may live to see you again,
but my days are numbered, whatever the lawyer may
say to the contrary."

Mary explained that Mr. Thorpe was waiting for
her, and saying that she was glad to hear he was to
have some one to attend on him, bade him good-bye.

During the drive to Triton Cottage the lawyer did
not further allude to Mr. Shank, and Mary very naturally forbore to question him.

Aunt Sally, who had become somewhat anxious at
her long absence, was greatly surprised at seeing Mr.
Thorpe, and not being influenced by the same motive
as Mary, inquired what the old man could possibly
have desired to see him about.

"To make his will, Miss Sally," answered the lawyer; "it has been signed, sealed, and delivered in the presence of myself and John Brown, my clerk, and its contents are to remain locked in our respective breasts and my strong box until the due time arrives for its administration. That he has made a will argues that he has, as you may suppose, some property to leave, and that the people in our neighbourhood were not so far wrong in calling him a miser; but he has hoarded to some purpose, and I wish that all misers would leave their gold in as satisfactory a manner as he has done."

In vain Miss Sally endeavoured to elicit further information; the lawyer laughed and rubbed his hands, but not a word more could she get out of him than he chose to say. Then turning the subject, he steadily declined again entering on it, though he made himself agreeable by conversing in a cheerful tone on various others.

Mary's anxiety prompted her to visit Mr. Shank the next day, and her aunt not objecting she set off by herself. A respectable-looking woman opened the door, and courtesied to her as she did so.

"How is Mr. Shank?" asked Mary.

"He is not worse than he was yesterday; he has been asking for you ever so many times, miss, and has made me go to the door to see if you were coming. He'll be main glad to see you. I have been working hard to make the house look a little tidy, but

it is in a sad mess ; it is a wonder the whole of it didn't
come down and crush the old man before this———"

The woman would have continued to run on in the
same strain had not Mary begged to be allowed to enter.
She found Mr. Shank seated in his arm-chair, looking,
as she thought, very pale and weak. He thanked her,
much in his usual way, for again coming to see him,
and for bringing him another of Miss Sally's puddings,
but Mary remarked that he no longer spoke of his
poverty.

"I wanted very much to see you, my dear," he
said, in a gentle tone, which contrasted greatly with
that in which he used formally to speak ; " but I don't
want listeners, Mrs. Mason, I will request you to
retire and busy yourself at the further end of the
house, or out of doors."

The old woman looked somewhat astonished, but
obeyed without replying.

Mary could not fail to be surprised at the tone
of authority in which he spoke, as if he had been
accustomed all his life to give directions to an
attendant.

"Mary," he said, as he sat with his hands clasped,
leaning back in his chair, and glancing half aside at
her fair countenance, as if a feeling of shame oppressed
him, "you have been my good angel. I owe you
much, more than I can ever repay. Had it not been
for you, I should have gone down to my grave a
miserable, wretched being, with no one to care for me ;

but you awoke me to a sense of better things. I have
not always been as I am now, but care and disappointment came upon me, and those I loved were lost
through my fault, by my hard treatment. I see it
now, but I thought then they were alone to blame. I
once had wealth, but it was dissipated almost, not all,
and I feared lest the remainder would be lost; then I
became what you have known me, a wretched, grovel-
ling miser. I had a daughter, she was young and fair,
and as bright as you are, but she desired to live as she
had been accustomed to, not aware of my losses, and
I stinted her of everything except the bare necessaries
of life. She had many admirers: one of them was
wealthy, but Fanny regarded him with dislike; the
other, a fine youth, was, I thought, penniless. She
returned his affection, and I ordered him never again to
enter my doors. My child bore my treatment meekly,
but one day she came into my presence, and in a calm
but firm voice said she would no longer be a burden to
me; that she was ready to toil for my support were it
requisite, but that she was well aware that I was possessed of ample means to obtain the comforts as well
as the necessaries of life. Enraged, I ordered her,
with a curse, to quit my house, declaring that I
would never see her again. She obeyed me too faithfully, and became the young man's wife, and she and
her husband left England. I heard shortly afterwards
that the ship in which they sailed had been wrecked.
That such was the case I had every reason to believe

as from that day I lost all trace of them. Hardhearted as I was, I believed that my child had met her just doom for the disobedience into which I myself had driven her, and having no one to care for, I sank into the wretched object you found me. You will think of me, Mary, with pity rather than scorn when I am gone?"

"Do not speak so, Mr. Shank; I have long, long pitied you," said Mary, soothingly. "You are not what you were; you mourn your past life, and you know the way by which you can be reconciled to a merciful God."

The old man gazed at her fair countenance. "No other human being could have moved me but you," he said ; "you reminded me from the first of my lost child, and I listened to you as I would have listened to no one else. Bless you ! bless you !"

Mary had already spent a longer time than she had intended listening to the old man's history. She rose to go away. He kept her small hand in his shrivelled palms.

"I should wish my last gaze on earth to be on your face, Mary; I should die more easily, and yet I do not fear death as I once did when I strove to put away all thoughts of it. I know it must come before long ; it may be days, or weeks, and you will then know how my poor wretched heart has loved you."

Mary, not understanding him, answered—

"You have shown me that already, Mr. Shank, and

I hope you may be spared to find something worth living for."

" Yes, if I had health and strength I should wish to assist in benefiting those poor Africans of whom you have so often told me, and putting an end to the fearful slave trade ; but I cannot recall my wasted days, and I must leave it to you, Mary. If you have the means to try and help them, you will do so, I know, far better than I can."

" I shall be thankful if I can ever benefit the poor Africans," said Mary, smiling at what appeared to her so very unlikely. " But I must stop no longer, or Aunt Sally will fancy that some harm has befallen me."

Mary wished him good-bye, summoning Mrs. Mason as she went out.

On Mary's return to Triton Cottage she found Lieutenant Meadows, who had come to wish her and her aunt good-bye, his turn of service on the coast-guard having expired.

He inquired whether they had received any news of the " Hope."

" She must have been round the Cape long ago. Hanson and his people should by this time have landed, so that you would get letters from the Cape, or perhaps even from Zanzibar, in the course of a week or two. You will write to me and say what news you receive in case Charley's letters should miscarry."

Miss Sally promised, without fail, to write as Mr.

Meadows requested, and he gave her his address. When he was gone, Miss Sally and Mary had no one to talk to on the subject nearest their hearts. They discussed it over and over again by themselves, in spite of Aunt Sally's declaration that it was of no use, and that they had better not speak about the matter; yet she was generally the first to begin, and Mary would bring out the map, and they both would pore over it, the elder lady through her spectacles, as if they could there discover by some magical power where Ned was, and the point the "Hope" had reached. They were cheerful and happy, though nothing occurred to vary the monotony of their every-day life, until the post one morning brought a letter addressed to Miss Sarah Pack.

"Whom can it be from?" she exclaimed, adjusting her spectacles. "It is not from my brother; it bears only the English post mark. Give me my scissors, Mary." And she deliberately cut it open, though not the less eager to know its contents.

Mary watched her as she read, holding the letter up to the light, and murmuring, "Astonishing!" "Very strange!" "I cannot understand it!" "And yet not impossible!" "I don't know whether I ought to tell you the contents of this," she said, after she had read it twice over; "it may agitate you, my dear Mary, and raise expectations only to be disappointed. It is from Mr. Farrance, and a very singular story he gives me."

These remarks could not fail to arouse Mary's curiosity.

"Is it about Ned? Has he been found? Is he coming back?" she exclaimed, her hand trembling in an unusual manner as she was about to pour out a cup of tea for her aunt.

"No, he does not give us any news of Ned. The letter has reference to you. I ought not to wish that anything to your advantage should not happen, but yet I almost dread lest Mr. Farrance's expectations should be realised."

"Oh, do tell me, aunt, what Mr. Farrance says!" exclaimed Mary. "I will nerve myself for whatever it may be; but I cannot even guess."

"Have you no suspicion on the subject?" asked Miss Sally, after a few moments' silence.

"None whatever," answered Mary.

Miss Sally looked at her earnestly with eyes full of affection, and then said, speaking very slowly—

"You know, my dear Mary, how my brother found you and Tom Baraka floating on a piece of wreck in the Indian Ocean, and how neither you nor Tom were able to give any account of yourselves—he not understanding English, and you being too young to remember what had occurred. From the day my brother brought you home we have ever loved you dearly, and supposing that your parents perished, we believed that no one would appear to take you away from us."

"Yes, indeed, dear aunt, and I have never wished to leave you," said Mary, in a gentle tone. "If Mr. Farrance wishes me to do so, pray tell him that it is impossible."

"There may be one who has a greater right to claim you than we have, and should he prove his claim, we should be unable to hold you from him."

"But how can any one have a claim upon me? I don't understand, aunt," said Mary, completely puzzled. "Pray tell me what Mr. Farrance does say."

"You shall hear his letter, and then judge for yourself, my dear child," said Miss Sally, and again holding the letter before her spectacles, she read—

"MY DEAR MISS PACK,—I lose no time in informing you during your good brother's absence of a circumstance which may possibly greatly affect your young charge Mary. I must tell you that I had a brother who, at an early age, having married imprudently, left England, and that I and the rest of his family long supposed him dead. Two days ago a gentleman, who said that he had just returned to this country after having resided for many years in one of the Dutch East India settlements, called upon me. After some conversation he inquired whether I suspected who he was, and, greatly to my astonishment, he announced himself as my long-lost brother He was so changed by

time and a pestiferous climate, and sorrow and trials
of all sorts, that I had a great difficulty in recognising
him, though I was at length satisfied that he was my
brother, and as such welcomed him home. While
he was yesterday evening narrating the events of his
life, he mentioned having sent his wife, whose health
required a change of climate, and their only child, a
little girl, on board a ship bound for the Cape of
Good Hope, where a correspondent of his house had
promised to receive them, but that the ship was lost
and that all on board, it was believed, had perished.
On hearing this it at once struck me as possible, and
remember I say barely possible, that the child picked
up by Lieutenant Pack might be my brother's daughter.
On comparing dates I found, as nearly as I can calculate, that they agree. Of course I do not forget that
there might have been several children of the same
age on board the ship. Even should the wreck Mr.
Pack fell in with have been a portion of the ill-fated
ship, yet some other child instead of my brother's
might have been saved. It would be difficult, but not
impossible, to identify her. My brother is more sanguine than I am on the subject, and is anxious to
come down with me as soon as his health will allow,
if you will give us permission, to see your young
charge. You may possibly have preserved the clothes
she had on and any ornaments about her which might
assist in her identification. Although my brother
might not be able to recognise them, he tells me that

a black girl, who was a nurse in his family and much attached to the child, is still alive, and he proposes to send for her immediately. He has married again and has a large family. Though Mary may be pleased to find that she has a number of brothers and sisters, her position as to fortune will not be greatly altered ; however on that point she will not concern herself as much as you and others, her elders, may possibly do, and we will take care that she is not the loser should the hopes we entertain be realised.

" I have written this, my dear madam, as you ought to receive the earliest information on the subject, and because you may think fit to prepare your young charge for what may otherwise prove so startling to her ; but I leave that to your judgment, and hoping in the course of a few days to see you,

         " I remain,

           " Yours faithfully,

             " J. FARRANCE."

Mary sat for some minutes, her hands clasped and apparently lost in thought, then she burst into tears, exclaiming, "My poor, poor mother ! I cannot help picturing her on the deck of the sinking ship, while the fierce waves were foaming around her until she was carried away and lost."

It was strange she did not think so much of her

supposed father and the new brothers and sisters she might find. Miss Sally endeavoured to calm her.

"My dear, dear Mary, I ought not to have read this letter to you," she exclaimed, "you must try to forget it; but I am afraid that you will not do that, and we must endeavour to wait patiently until Mr. Farrance and his brother appear. They may find that they are mistaken, and then you will still be my little niece, and as much loved as ever."

Mary soon grew calm, and tried to follow Miss Sally's advice by waiting patiently for the appearance of their expected visitors. We, in the meantime, must go to a far off part of the world.

CHAPTER IX.

N O one will suppose that Ned Garth was
dead, more than did his loving friends,
although a long time had elapsed, and
no tidings of him had been received.

When ordered by Mr. Rhymer to try and
prevent the escape of the slaves, he sprang forward without thinking of the risk he ran. He
had succeeded in getting in front of a large party
of the fugitives, endeavouring by all the significant
gestures he could think of to induce them to turn
back to the shore, when he was felled to the ground
by a blow from behind. He retained sufficient con-
sciousness, however, to be aware that he had been
picked up and was being dragged along rapidly in the
midst of a crowd of blacks. He could hear at first
the shouts of his shipmates, but they gradually
became less and less distinct. He felt that he was
being carried forward further and further from the
river, sometimes completely lifted off his feet. He
could not, fortunately for himself, collect his scattered

senses sufficiently to consider what would probably be
his fate. His first idea, when he recovered from the
blow, was the desire to try and escape, but he had
neither the strength nor opportunity to get away. When
he opened his eyes he saw a number of black faces
scowling round him, and several well-dressed Arabs
a little distance off, while on every side were other
negroes being driven in like a flock of terrified sheep
to a common centre. Presently a much larger party
of Arabs than those who had formed the crew of the
dhow made their appearance, and were welcomed with
shouts of satisfaction.

The whole party now occupied themselves in bind-
ing the negroes, some with ropes round their necks
and others with forked sticks, a treatment to which
they appeared to submit without resistance. The
blacks who guarded Ned were apparently free men,
or at all events attached to the Arabs. They
jabbered away and made signs, intimating that he
was soon to be put to death; he prepared himself
therefore for what he had too much reason to fear
would be his fate. He knew that it would be useless
to ask for mercy. Had he been able to speak their
tongue, he would have told them that they would
gain much more by delivering him up to his friends;
but, as his arms were kept tight, he could not even
make signs to that effect. He waited therefore, with
as much calmness as he could command, for what
would next follow. Several of the slaves had in the

meantime attempted to escape, but were pursued by the Arabs and some of the free blacks. The least active, or those who had last started, were soon brought back; he heard, however, shots fired, and after a time the pursuers returned dragging along those they had recovered, two of whom were bleeding from gun-shot wounds in the shoulders. Whether any had been killed he could not then learn, but he afterwards ascertained that three had been shot as a warning to the rest. The slaves having at length been secured, the party moved forward towards the west, keeping the river in sight on their right hand. As evening approached, they encamped at some distance from the bank. Fires were lighted, but no food was cooked—for the best of all reasons, that the party were destitute of provisions. Ned observed that armed sentries were placed round the camp, but that was probably to prevent any of the slaves escaping rather than on account of an expected attack.

He had some faint hope that Rhymer might have got back to the ship in time to give information of what had happened, and that the boats might be sent up to attempt his re-capture. At length, overcome with fatigue, he lay down between the two blacks who had him in charge, and in spite of the disagreeable proximity of his guards, he was soon fast asleep; his slumbers, however, were troubled, but he continued dozing on until he was aroused by the Arabs summoning their followers to re-commence the march.

Water had been brought from the river, but they started without food, and it was not till late in the day that, reaching a village, they compelled the inhabitants to supply them by threatening to burn their huts if they refused. Ultimately, crossing the river by a ford, they proceeded for some distance towards the north.

Ned did not fail to be on the watch for an opportunity of escaping; he thought that if he could hide himself away he might get down to the coast, and have a chance of falling in with one of the boats. He was, however, far too closely guarded, he discovered, for this to be possible. He was still unable to conjecture for what object the Arabs had carried him off. For three days they journeyed on, the whole party suffering greatly from want of food, and sometimes from thirst, when long stretches of barren ground were passed over without a drop of water to be found. At last he discovered that they were directing their course once more to the eastward, and in another day they came in sight of the sea. There was a high cliff on the right hand, sheltering a deep bay in which three dhows rode at anchor. On a signal being made the dhows stood in towards the inner part of the bay, where a small creek formed a harbour of sufficient size to contain them, so that they were able to moor close to the shore. Several Arabs landed from each of them. After the preliminary salaams had been gone through, business at once commenced, which terminated apparently in a bargain being struck for the purchase of the whole party of slaves, their price consisting of bales of cloth, coils of wire, beads, and other articles, which were at once landed; and this being done, the slaves were shipped on board the dhows. Ned almost hoped that he might be sent with them, as he thought that he might thus have a better opportunity of making his escape than he could expect to find should he be detained by his captors. He was greatly disappointed, therefore, on finding that he was still kept a prisoner. He looked seaward with a longing gaze, thinking it possible that either the ship or the boats might appear in search of the dhows; but not seeing them, he guessed that the cunning Arabs had taken the opportunity of shipping the slaves while they remained off the mouth of the river. Several other Arabs had joined their party, which now consisted of thirty well-armed men, besides nearly one hundred pagazis, or carriers, hired from the neighbouring villages to convey the goods into the interior. Among them was a finely-dressed individual wearing on his head a large turban, and round his waist a rich scarf, into which were stuck a dagger and a brace of silver-mounted pistols. He appeared to take the lead, and Ned discovered that he was called Mohammed-ibn-Nassib. He had not long joined the party when his eye fell on Ned. Pointing towards him he inquired who the young stranger was. The answer he received appeared to satisfy him, and he turned away without making any further remark. The party being marshalled the march began, the Arabs keeping a strict watch on the blacks carrying their goods.

At nightfall they halted near the banks of a stream which evidently fell into the main river. As Ned observed its course, the thought occurred to him that if he could find a canoe, or for want of one a log of timber, he might float down with the current and reach the boats, which he felt sure would be sent to look for him. To do this, however, he must first elude his guards, who were, he found to his satisfaction, less watchful than at first, being apparently satisfied that he would not attempt to escape.

It was terribly trying work to be alone, without any one to speak to who understood a word he said. Several fires were lighted in the camp, which served both for cooking provisions and scaring away the wild beasts. Ned was allowed to sit near one, round which Mohammed and the other Arabs collected. Hoping to throw them off their guard, he assumed as unconcerned an air as possible, endeavouring to make them believe that he was reconciled to his lot. He was still as much in the dark as ever as to what they intended to do with him. Their purpose could scarcely be to sell him as a slave, but possibly they thought that by exhibiting him as a prisoner to the black chiefs they might gain the credit of having defeated the English.

In a short time their evening meal was brought by the attendants, one of whom, when they were served, placed a bowl of rice, seasoned with red pepper and salt, before him. It was the food the slaves were fed upon. Though aware of this, he was too hungry to refuse it, and trying to look perfectly satisfied, he ate up the rice as if it was exactly the dish he preferred, and then put out the bowl to ask for more.

Mohammed shook his head to signify that he must be content with the share given him, while the rest seemed highly amused with his look of disappointment. After some time they retired to sleep in some rude huts, which their attendants had put up for them, when he was led away by his two watchful guards. He was placed as usual between them, and lay down, covering himself up with a piece of matting which one of the Arabs more kindly disposed than the rest had given him. Drawing the matting over his head, he pretended to go to sleep, but he kept his eye at a hole, through which he could partially see what was taking place.

He waited for some time watching his guards until their loud snores assured him that their slumbers were not feigned, and at length all sounds having ceased in the camp, he cautiously lifted up his head to ascertain whether any sentries had been placed near him, but he could see none either on the one side or the other. The fires had burnt low. "Some one will soon come to wake them up," he thought; "it will be imprudent to move yet." He waited for some time longer, but the flames got lower and lower, and at last the glare they had thrown on the neighbouring trees faded away.

"Now or never is my time to escape," he said to himself. Creeping out from under his mat, which he left raised up in the centre to appear as if he was still beneath it, he crawled along for some distance on his hands and knees. He stopped, however, every now and then to ascertain if any sentry, who might have been lying down, had risen to his feet and was likely to discover him. Thus advancing a few yards at a time, he made his way towards the river. His intention was then to continue down along it until he could find a canoe. He had nearly gained the water when cries, shrieks, and loud shouts reached his ear, followed by the sound of firearms. Several bullets came whistling close to his head; to avoid them he sprang behind the trunk of a large tree. Scarcely had he done so, when he heard close to him the crash of bushes, and a huge animal bounded by carrying in its jaws what, seen through the gloom, appeared to be the dead body of a man. He heard a faint cry as if from a human voice, followed by the continued crash of the underwood as the creature rushed along the very course he had intended to pursue. Hardly had it disappeared than the cries and shouts, growing nearer and nearer, showed him that a number of men from the camp were coming in pursuit of the animal, and that he could scarcely avoid being discovered. Even if this should happen, he had reason to be thankful that he had not attempted

to make his escape sooner, or he would in all pro
bability have met the lion and fallen a victim instead
of the man who had been carried off. He crouched
down among the thick roots of the tree, hoping that
even now he might not be discovered; at the same
time he felt that it would be madness to attempt to
pursue the course he had intended down the river, as
he should in all probability, if he did so, encounter
the lion which had carried off the man. He waited, his
heart.beating quickly. The blacks came on, shouting
at the top of their voices to keep up their courage and
to frighten the lion, but did not discover him. He
must now decide what to do, either to return to the
camp and wait for another opportunity or to continue
his flight. Every day would increase his distance
from the coast and the difficulties he must encounter
to reach it. The thought occurred to him that he
might cross the river and go down on the opposite
bank, though he did not fail to remember that crocodiles or hippopotami might be lying concealed in its
bed, but he resolved to run the risk rather than again
place himself in the power of the Arabs. Not a
moment was to be lost. He sprang from his place of
concealment and ran towards the bank. Scarcely had
he reached it than he heard the men coming back,
shouting as before to each other, for they had not
ventured to follow the lion far, knowing that their
companion must by that time have been dead. He
did not therefore hesitate. Slipping into the water,

he struck out across the stream. He had got nearly
half way over, when he became aware that the shouts
he heard were directed at him. Not daring to look
back, he swam on with all his strength, hoping that
no one would venture to follow him.

On and on he went. Thoughts of crocodiles and
hippopotami would intrude, but he trusted that the
noise made by the blacks would drive them away. No
shots were fired at him. Why this was he could not
tell—perhaps he was no longer seen. Then the idea
occurred that some one might be pursuing him; still,
undaunted, he continued his course. Reeds flanked
the opposite bank of the stream; should he be able to
force his way through them? If he could, they would
afford him concealment. He could distinguish them
rising up like a wall before him; he at last reached
them, and began to struggle through the barrier. It
was hard work, for the water was still too deep to
allow him to wade, and the reeds bent down as he
clutched them; still, as those he first grasped yielded,
he seized others, and hauled himself along. At length
his feet touched the bottom, and he was able to make
somewhat better progress. He had not time to consider what he should do when he had gained the firm
ground. There might be other lions in the way, but
he resolved not to be deterred by the fear of encounter-
ing them; he dreaded far more falling into the hands
of the Arabs. He expected every moment to reach
the shore, when one of his feet stuck fast in the mud.

He endeavoured to obtain a firmer foothold by pressing down the reeds so that he might stand upon them, but this caused considerable delay, and in his efforts he was nearly falling on his face into the water. At length he succeeded in drawing out his foot, and once more he struggled on. The noise made by the bending reeds had prevented him from hearing a loud rustling at no great distance which now struck his ear. It might be caused by one of the huge inhabitants of the river. Should an hippopotamus have discovered him, he must seek for safety by climbing the nearest tree he could reach. The idea incited him to fresh exertions. He sprang forward, his hand touched the firm ground. He drew himself up the bank, but was so exhausted by his efforts that he had scarcely strength sufficient to run for a tree. As he stood for a few moments endeavouring to recover himself, he fixed on one a short distance off, a branch of which hung down sufficiently low to enable him to swing himself up by it. He took one glance also behind him. The darkness prevented him from seeing the figures of the Arabs on the opposite side, but he could hear their voices still shouting loudly. Having recovered his breath, he once more started off in the direction of the tree. Should he there find that he was not pursued, as he expected, he intended to continue his course along the bank of the river. He reached the tree, and was on the point of grasping the bough when he heard men shouting behind him, and, glancing over his shoulder, he distinguished amid the gloom three dark figures coming on at full speed. He hoped, however, that he might not have been seen, and that, if he could once get into the tree, they might pass by. He made frantic efforts to draw himself up, and had just succeeded when he felt his foot seized by a human hand. He in vain endeavoured to free himself. The gruff voice of a black shouted to him, and he recognised it as that of one of his former guards. The man pulled away at his leg with such force that he was compelled to let go his hold, and would have fallen heavily to the ground had not his other pursuers, who came up, caught him. Once more he found himself a prisoner. His captors, he judged by the way they spoke, were abusing him, though he could not understand what they said. Further resistance was useless, so he resigned himself to his fate. What they were going to do with him he could not tell; whether they would recross the river or remain on the side he had reached. They led him down to the bank, from which a large amount of shouting was exchanged. This finally ceased, and he found himself being led up the stream, as he concluded, towards a ford, or to some spot where a crossing might be more easily effected than at the place where he had swum over. He was right in his conjectures, for after some time torches appeared on the opposite side, and his captors, dragging him along, plunged into the stream, and began to wade across, shouting and shrieking at the top of their voices as they did so, and beating the water with some long sticks to drive away the crocodiles. Several Arabs and blacks with torches received the party as they landed, casting scowling looks at poor Ned, who had abundance of abuse heaped upon him for his futile attempt to escape. On being léd back to the camp, however, he was allowed to dry his wet clothes before the fire, which he did by taking some of them off at a time.

It was a sore trial to him to be all alone without any human being to whom he could speak. At last the blacks led him back to the very spot from which he had escaped, and he was allowed to cover himself up again with his mat. He saw, however, that one of the men was sitting by his side to keep watch.

He was too much exhausted to think over his disappointment, or to fear any evil consequences from remaining so long wet. He soon fell into a deep slumber, from which he was aroused by one of the blacks shaking him by the shoulder, while another brought a bowl of rice and a cup of coffee.

On looking round he perceived that the caravan was preparing to march. The pagazis had shouldered their loads, and the Arabs were girding themselves for the journey. Knowing that he would have to accompany them, he got up ready to obey the summons to move. He was surprised to see Mohammed, the leader, approaching him. The Arab chief spoke a few words, laughing heartily, slapped him on the shoulder in a familiar way, and Ned concluded that he was complimenting him on the manner he had attempted his escape. He then lifted his gun as if about to shoot, and put it into his hands, making signs that he was to use it, and Ned surmised that it was intended he should fight for the Arabs.

After this Mohammed seemed much more friendly than before, and invited him frequently to march by his side. The river was crossed by the ford, and the caravan proceeded westward.

Ned cast many a lingering look behind as he got further and further from the stream by means of which he had hoped to rejoin his friends. He was too strictly watched, however, to have the slightest chance of escaping. The country near the coast had been almost depopulated, and very few villages or habitations of any description were passed. As the caravan advanced more people were met with, and several large villages were seen, to the chiefs of some of which the Arabs paid a sort of tribute in beads and wire, and occasionally cloth, for the sake of retaining their friendship.

Shortly afterwards they were joined by another caravan, containing even more men than their own, and together they formed a large party. He was introduced formally to the new-comers, who seemed to look at him with much interest and treat him with respect. Though allowed to wander in the neighbourhood of the camp he found that one of the blacks was always strictly watching him, and that even had he intended to escape he should have no opportunity of so doing. He now observed that the Arabs marched more cautiously than heretofore, that scouts were sent out and returned frequently to report what was going on in front. At last one day the caravan halted earlier than usual, and the pagazis were immediately set to work to cut down young trees, with which stockades were formed round the camp, and every man remained under arms. The Arab leaders, seated on carpets outside their huts, held long consultations. which, though Ned attended them, he was unable to understand a word that was said. He guessed, however, from their gestures and the expression of their countenances, that some were counselling peace and others war—that the advice of the latter prevailed he judged from the excited tones of their voices, while the chiefs touched the hilts of their swords, or drew them from their scabbards and flourished them in the air. The opinion he came to from all he heard and saw was that some potentate or other, through whose country they desired to pass, had prohibited their progress, and that they had determined to force their onward way in spite of his opposition. That many of the chiefs had for some time been prepared for this Ned was convinced from the preparations they had made.

Leaving a garrison within the camp to guard their goods, the next morning the little army commenced its march, each chief dressed in his gayest attire, attended by a lad carrying his gun, drums beating, colours flying, and musical instruments emitting strange sounds, while the black followers of the Arabs chanted their various war songs in discordant tones. Mohammed had sent for Ned, and by signs made him understand that he was to be his armour-bearer, and to accompany him to battle. Ned was very much inclined to decline the honour. He questioned whether the Arabs had any right to insist on marching through a country claimed by others. Whatever quarrel might exist it was no concern of his. Then came the point, should he refuse, he would be looked upon with contempt and treated as a slave, and would have less chance of escaping; as to the danger, it did not enter into his calculations. "The Arab insists on my accompanying him, and will make me promise to fight, so fight I must," he thought. "I do not see how I can help myself." He therefore nodded and patted the gun handed him, showing that he knew well how to use it. The chiefs marched forward in high spirits, congratulating each other beforehand on the victory they expected to achieve. Ned kept by Mohammed's side, carrying the chief's gun as well as his own, an honour he would gladly have dispensed with.

About noon the force halted to dine, and two hours afterwards they came in sight, from the top of slightly elevated ground, of a stockaded enclosure, the interior filled with huts on the side of a gentle slope. The chiefs pointed towards it and addressed their followers, who replied with loud shouts. Ned guessed that it was the place about to be attacked. No other enemies had been seen, and the village did not appear capable of holding out against so formidable a force. The Arabs, expecting to gain an easy victory, advanced in loose order to the attack. While one party rushed at the gate to break it open, the remainder halting fired their muskets, but as the stockades were thick no injury was inflicted on the garrison. Not a missile was shot in return. Emboldened by this they were advancing close up to the stockade, when suddenly a shower of bullets, accompanied by a flight of arrows, came whistling about their heads. Several of the attacking party fell dead, pierced through and through, two or three of the chief Arabs being among them, while others were badly wounded.

Mohammed, taking his gun from Ned's hand and shouting his battle cry, rushed forward, firing as he advanced. In the meantime the gate had been opened. Many of the Arabs and a large number of their followers sprang in. No resistance was offered. Others were about to follow when the gate was shut, and directly afterwards the sharp rattle of musketry was heard, mingled with the shouts of the Arabs and the shrieks and cries of the negroes, but not a shot was fired at those outside. Then there came an ominous silence. Suddenly it was broken by renewed firing, but this time the shots were directed towards

the assailants, who were still pressing on to the walls.
In vain they attempted to force the gate, numbers
were falling; already half their number, with those
cut to pieces inside the village, were killed or
wounded, and Mohammed, calling his followers round
him, retreated, leaving all the dead and many of the
worst wounded behind to the mercy of the victors.
They hurried on until they were beyond the range of
the muskets of the fort, when they halted, and
Mohammed asked whether they would renew the
attack and revenge the loss of their friends or retreat.

The point was settled by the appearance of a band
of black warriors armed, some with shields and spears
and others with muskets, issuing from the gate.

The retreat was continued, and Mohammed had
the greatest difficulty in preventing it from becoming
a disorganised flight. Bravely he faced about, and
setting the example to his men fired his musket at
the advancing foe; but the latter, halting when the
Arabs stopped, kept out of range, again advancing
as soon as they moved on.

Ned remaine . with Mohammed, who shook his head
mournfully as if acknowledging his defeat. He had
reason to look grave. The distance to the camp was
great, they were in an enemy's country, and there
was more than one defile to pass through, while the
thick woods and tall grass on either side might conceal large bodies of their foes. Again and again the
Arab called on his men to keep together, and not to

be disheartened, though he himself showed his apprehensions by the expression of his countenance. For a couple of hours the retreating force had marched on, the dark band of savages hovering in their rear, but not venturing near enough to come to blows.

Mohammed continued to cast anxious glances on either hand, and retained his musket instead of giving it back to Ned to carry for him. Ned longed to be able to ask him what hope there was of getting back safe to the camp, but when he made signs the chief only gave in return an ominous shake of the head.

One of the defiles they had to pass through was entered, Mohammed gazed round even more anxiously than before, scanning every rock and bush which might conceal a foe. While their pursuers were still in sight, the narrowest part was gained. The chief had inspired Ned with his own apprehensions, and every moment he expected to be assailed by a shower of arrows and javelins. He breathed more freely when they once more entered the open country. As they advanced they looked behind, hoping that the negroes would not have ventured through the pass, but they were still pursuing. The Arabs dared not halt to rest or take any refreshment, for it was all-important to reach their camp before nightfall. Once there, as it was well stored with provisions, they might wait for reinforcements.

A thick wood, however, was before them and another rocky defile. As they approached the wood,

Mohammed again showed his anxiety. Several of the men now gave in, the wounded especially suffered greatly, and one by one they dropped, no attempt being made to carry them on. The wood, however, was passed, and next the defile appeared. Their figures cast long shadows on the ground, and the entrance to the gorge looked dark and threatening. The fugitives were too much fatigued to climb the heights to ascertain if any foes lurked among them. "On, on!" was the cry, Mohammed and the other chiefs leading. Ned cast one look behind, and saw that the negroes were pressing forward in their rear at a faster pace than before; the move was ominous. The pass was entered. The men went on at a sharp run, each eager to get through. Not a shout was uttered, the tramp of many feet alone was heard, when suddenly the comparative silence was broken by fierce shrieks and cries, and from all sides came showers of arrows and javelins, while from the heights above their heads rushed down a complete avalanche of rocks and stones. Ned saw Mohammed pierced through by an arrow; all the other chiefs the next instant shared the same fate. There was no hope of escaping by pushing forward, as the path was barred by a band of shrieking savages, while on every side lay the dead or dying, crushed by stones or pierced by arrows and darts. In the rear he could distinguish the few survivors endeavouring to cut their way out by the road they had come, fighting desperately

with the band of warriors who had pursued them, but
they too were quickly brought to the ground, and not
half a dozen of his companions remained standing.
He was looking round to see whether any overhang-
ing rock or hollow would afford him shelter, when a
stone struck his head and he sank almost senseless
to the ground. The next instant the savages in
front came rushing on, while others, descending from
the heights, leapt into the ravine. He gave himself
up for lost. The savages sprang forward, uttering
cries more of terror than victory. No one attempted
to strike the fallen. Some climbed up the rocks,
others rushed at headlong speed through the ravine.
The cause was evident, they were being pursued. A
rattling fire was opened upon them, the bullets striking either the rocks or the ground close to where Ned
lay, he being partly protected, however, by the bodies
of the Arab chiefs, none hit him. The savages continued their flight until they joined the party at the
western end of the pass. Here they turned about,
encouraged by their friends, to meet the fresh body of
Arabs. A fierce fight now took place, and the Arabs
had cause to repent their imprudence in so hurriedly
pushing forward. Several of their leaders fell, and
they in their turn retreated. Ned saw them coming,
and at the same time he observed that a number of
the savages had again climbed the heights and were
preparing to assail them as they had Mohammed's
party. Fortunately for the Arabs, the Africans had

expended most of their missiles. Ned implored the
first who passed in their retreat to lift him up and to
carry him with them, for he fully expected to be
trampled to death should he not be killed by the
falling rocks or the arrows of the savages. His cries
were unheeded; already the greater number had
passed by, when he saw an Arab, evidently a chief,
bringing up the rear, and encouraging the men under
him by continuing their fire to keep the foe in check.
Ned recognised him as the Arab whose life he had
saved from the sinking dhow.

"Sayd, Sayd!" he shouted, "don't you know
me? Do help me out of this."

"Yes, yes, I will save you," answered the Arab.
There was no time for further words and stooping
down Sayd lifted Ned in his arms and, with the aid
of one of his followers, bore him on through the
pass, while his men, as before, kept their pursuers at
bay.

The open country was at length gained. The
savages, although they might rightly claim the victory, having suffered severely, showed no inclination
to continue the pursuit.

Of the whole force, however, which had marched
out in the morning with Mohammed not a dozen
remained alive, and most of those were badly
wounded. Ned was unable to speak to Sayd until
the fortified camp was gained. No sooner had they
arrived than their ears were deafened by the wailing

cries of the women mourning for their husbands and relatives slain, and it was some time before Ned could obtain the rest he so much required after the injury he had received and the fatigues he had gone through.

CHAPTER X.

FTER resting some time Ned recovered sufficiently to converse with Sayd, who, coming up, seated himself by his side.

"I had heard that a young white man had set out with Mohammed-ibn-Nassib, and was acting as his gun-bearer, but little did I expect to find that you were the person spoken of. How came you to be with him? Have you run away from your ship?" he inquired.

"No, indeed," answered Ned; and he explained how he had been made prisoner and ill-treated, until Mohammed took him into his service. "And how came you to be here?" asked Ned. "Surely you have not joined company with these men-stealers?"

"Men-stealers! O no; my friends and I are on an expedition to purchase elephant tusks from the natives far away in the interior, where they are so plentiful that people make their door-posts of them, and we all expect to become immensely rich."

"I hope that you will succeed," said Ned; "but I would rather have heard that you were returning to the coast, that I might accompany you, as I am very desirous of getting back to my ship. Can you, however, assist me?"

"You ask what is impossible. If you attempt to go alone, you will be murdered by the robbers through whose territory we have passed. No white men can travel among these savages, unless in considerable numbers well armed. If we meet with a caravan on its way seaward you may put yourself under its protection; but I should be sorry, now we have met, to part with you, and would advise you to accompany us until we have accomplished our undertaking."

"I thank you for the offer; but, if it is possible, I must go back to my ship," said Ned.

"But I say that it is impossible," answered Sayd, who evidently did not wish to part with Ned. "Make up your mind to come with us, and you shall receive a portion of my share of the profits of the expedition."

Ned again thanked Sayd, adding—

"But I have no goods with which to trade, and I would not deprive you of your gains. My captain will, however, I am sure, repay any one for the expenses of my journey."

"But you can do without goods; you have Mohammed's musket, and with it you may shoot some elephants; besides which, it is just possible that we may have to attack some villages if the inhabitants refuse to supply us with tusks or provisions. It is very likely that some will do so, in which case you will have a right to the booty we may obtain."

"I thought, friend Sayd, that you were going on a hunting and trading expedition ? "

" It is the Arabs' way of trading when the negroes are obstinate," answered Sayd, with a laugh.

Ned, on hearing this, became somewhat suspicious of the intentions of the Arabs, but he feared he should be unable to help himself. He resolved, however, that should an opportunity offer, to get back to the coast at all risks.

The caravan to which Sayd belonged was far larger than that of Mohammed. It was under the command of a magnificent fellow in appearance, Habib-ibn-Abdullah, to whom his followers looked with reverential awe. There were numerous other chiefs, each attended by fifty or more black free men or slaves, some armed with muskets or swords, and the rest with spears and knives, or bows and arrows. Sayd had about fifty of these men under his orders, entrusted to him by his father and other relatives at Zanzibar.

The caravan waited in the entrenched camp, expecting every hour to be attacked; but the negro chiefs had gained information of the number of the garrison, and thought it wiser not to make the attempt, intending probably to way-lay the caravan on its march, and cut it off should an opportunity occur.

Several days passed by ; no enemy appearing, **Abdullah**, mustering his men, ordered the march to begin. With drums beating, colours flying, and trumpets sounding, they marched out in gallant array, the armed men guarding the pagazis, who carried the bales of cloth, boxes of beads, and coils of wire. Though they looked so formidable, Ned, after the disgraceful defeat suffered by Mohammed, did not feel that confidence which he might otherwise have experienced. To avoid the defiles which had proved so disastrous to their friends, Abdullah took a course to the northward, which, after being pursued for a couple of days, was changed to the westward. Ned looked out anxiously in the hopes of meeting a return caravan ; still none appeared, and he was convinced that it would be madness to attempt returning by himself without the means of even paying for his food. Sayd was as kind and attentive as he could desire, generally marching alongside him, when they managed to converse freely together, the young Arab eking out his English by signs. A strict watch was kept night and day for enemies, but none ventured to attack them. Abdullah, however, consented to pay tribute to the various chiefs through whose territory the caravan passed. It consisted of so many yards of cloth, with a string or two of beads or several lengths of wire. Although muskets, powder, and shot were in demand, the Arabs refused to part with them, suspecting that the weapons might be turned against themselves when any difficulty might arise. The country of the more warlike tribes having been passed, the Arabs marched with less caution than before, their hunters being sent out to kill game, which appeared in great abundance — elephants, giraffes, buffalo, wild boars, zebras, and deer of various species, besides guinea-fowl, pelicans, and numerous other birds.

Ned had a great inclination to join these hunting parties, but Sayd persuaded him to remain in camp, indeed, on most occasions, he felt too much fatigued to take any unnecessary exercise.

An ample supply of meat put the caravan in good spirits, and they marched on, shouting and singing, feeling themselves capable of conquering the world.

"We have now a country before us very different to any we have yet traversed," observed Sayd. "The slaves will not sing quite so loudly."

They had just arrived at a small stream. Here Abdullah issued the order that every man should fill his water-bottle.

"We will carry a gourd apiece in addition, it will be well worth while bearing the extra weight, for before many days are over we shall esteem a few drops of water of as great value as so many pieces of gold," observed Sayd. "See how leaden the sky looks yonder, and how the air seems to dance over the surface of the earth."

Some of the chiefs desired to camp where they were,

but Abdullah was eager to push on, as they had marched but two hours that morning. A water-hole, he said, would be found before nightfall, or the people might dig and the precious fluid would be discovered beneath the earth.

After a short halt, therefore, they recommenced their march. The chiefs, who did not carry even their own muskets, found it easy enough, but the pagazis groaned under their heavy loads as they tramped over the baked ground. Scarcely a tree was to be seen, and such shrubs and plants only as require little water. The sun sinking towards the horizon appeared like a ball of fire, setting the whole western sky ablaze. Not a breath of air fanned the cheeks of the weary men. Ned did not complain, but he felt dreadfully tired, and had to apply so frequently to his gourd that it was nearly empty.

"We have not yet got half way over the desert," observed Sayd. "I advise you, my friend, to husband that precious liquid."

"But Abdullah believes that there is a water-hole before us."

"His belief will not bring it there!" answered Sayd. "It may by this time be dried up, and we may have many a long mile to march before we reach another."

A few minutes after this a line of trees appeared ahead. The blacks raised a shout of joy, supposing that beneath their shade the looked-for water would be discovered. Worn out as many of them were, they hastened their steps until even the carriers broke into a run, and the whole mass rushed eagerly down the bank, but as they reached the bottom a cry of bitter disappointment escaped them; not a drop of liquid was to be seen, only a smooth mass of black mud, with cracks across in all directions, showing that the water had evaporated.

Water must be had at every cost, or the whole party might perish. Their numbers, their arms, their courage would not avail them. Those who had before traversed the country immediately set to work with pointed sticks to dig along the bed of what was once a stream, in the hopes of obtaining water, and many dug holes of five and six feet deep, but no water appeared.

"Then, men, you must dig deeper," shouted the chiefs as they went about among their people.

A little thick liquid bubbled up, the labourers shouted with joy, and several of the more thirsty rushed in, and kneeling down lapped it up, although it was of the consistency of mud.

The men again set to work, and at length a sufficient quantity of water came bubbling up to enable their companions to obtain a few mouthfuls. The camp fires were then lit, and the men gathered close round them, for it was a locality where a prowling lion was very likely to pay them a visit.

Sayd and Ned had a sufficient amount of water to

prevent them suffering. As Ned looked out over the
dark plain, he could see objects flitting by. Sayd
thought that they were deer, which, fleet of foot, were
passing across the desert to some more fertile region.
Several times the roars of lions were heard, but none
ventured near the camp, being scared by the bright
blaze kept up.

At an early hour all were again on foot, and eagerly
descended into the holes, which now contained rather
more water than on the previous evening, but still
barely sufficient to quench their thirst. There was
none to fill their water-bottles. The Arabs, kneeling
on their carpets, joined by the Mohammedans among
their followers, offered up their prayers to Allah as
the first gleam of the sun rose above the horizon ;
then the morning meal being hastily taken, the
pagazis shouldered their loads and the march commenced.

As Sayd had predicted, no songs, no shouts were
heard ; even the merriest among the blacks were
silent. Scarcely a word was uttered as the caravan
moved forward, the dull sound of human feet treading
the baked earth alone broke the silence. On and on
they trudged ; the sun, as he rose, got hotter and
hotter, striking down with intense force on their
heads. Ned marched alongside Sayd. The latter
had two favoured followers—young Hassan, partly of
Arab birth, who acted as his gun-bearer ; and a huge
negro, a freed man, Sambroko by name, possessed of

prodigious strength and courage. These two had followed their master's example, and supplied themselves with gourds of water, two of which the negro carried slung round his neck.

For some hours the caravan proceeded as rapidly as at first. It was hoped that a stream would be found soon after noon, where Abdullah promised to halt to give the men the rest they so much needed ; but noon was passed, already the sun was in their eyes, and no stream was seen. To halt now would be to lose precious time. With parched lips and starting eyeballs the men pushed on, and, instead of songs and jokes, cries and groans were heard on every side. Now a weary pagazi sank down, declaring that he could carry his load no longer ; now another and another followed his example. In vain the Arab leaders urged them to rise with threats and curses, using the points of their spears. The hapless men staggered on, then dropping their loads attempted to fly. Two were shot dead as a warning to the rest, and their masters distributed their loads among the others who appeared better able to carry them, but, ere long, others sinking down, stretched themselves on the ground and were left to die in the desert. Time would have been lost in attempting to carry them.

" Is this the way you Arabs treat your followers ? " asked Ned, who felt indignant at the apparent cruelty of the chiefs.

" They are but slaves," answered Sayd in a careless

tone. "Necessity has no law; let us go forward, or their fate may be ours."

"Onwards, onwards!" was the cry. The chiefs shouted to their people to keep together, for already many were straggling behind. They had started, feeling confident that by their numbers all difficulties would be overcome, but had they mustered ten thousand men the same fate by which they were now threatened might have overtaken them. Even young Hassan, generally so joyous and dauntless, began to complain; but Sambroko took him by the arm and helped him along, every now and then applying his water-bottle to his lips.

Among the pagazis Ned had observed a young man of pleasing countenance, who had always been amongst the merriest of the merry, though his load was heavier than that of many. He had never complained, but was now staggering along endeavouring to keep up with the rest. Ned, seeing how much he was suffering, offered him a draught from his own water bottle.

"Stop!" cried Sayd. "You will want it for yourself."

"I cannot disappoint him," answered Ned, as he poured the water down the lad's throat.

The young pagazi's countenance brightened, and he uttered an expression of gratitude as he again attempted to follow his companions.

"I should like to carry some of his load," said Ned. "He is younger than the rest, and it is too much for him. Here! let me help you along," he added, making signs of his intention.

"You will bring contempt on yourself if you do that," observed Sayd. "No Arab would demean himself by carrying a load."

"An Englishman thinks nothing derogatory when necessary," answered Ned, taking the package off the shoulders of the youth, who, while he expressed his gratitude, seemed much astonished at the offer being made.

Ned trudged on with it manfully for some minutes, but soon began to feel the weight oppressive. Sambroko observed him, and, taking hold of the load, swung it on his own back and carried it a considerable distance. Then calling to the young pagazi bade him carry it forward.

Ned begged Sayd to thank Sambroko, who answered, that though he could no longer bear to see his master's friend thus fatigue himself, the young pagazi must expect no further help from him.

"But I must try and help him, for I could not bear to see the poor fellow sink down and die as so many are doing."

"There is nothing strange in that," remarked Sambroko. "I once crossed a desert larger than this, and one half our number were left behind; but we got through and returned during the wet season with large cargoes of ivory, and our masters, for I was then a slave, were well content."

Sayd translated to Ned what was said.

"I wonder the Arabs venture into a country where so many lose their lives," said Ned.

"The profits are great," answered Sayd. "Men will dare and do anything for gain; each hopes to be more fortunate than his predecessor."

The young slave, greatly rested and refreshed by the water, and even more by the sympathy shown him, marched forward with an almost elastic step.

"O young master!" he said, looking at Ned, "my heart feels light. I thought no one cared for poor Chando; but I now know that there are kind men in the world."

Sayd explained the meaning of the black's words.

"Chando!" repeated Ned. "I have heard that name before. Inquire where he comes from, and how long he has been a slave."

Sayd put the questions.

"From the village of Kamwawi in Warua," answered the young pagazi without hesitation. "It is far, far away from here. It is so long ago since I was taken that I could not find my way back; but were I once there, I should know it again. The hills around it, the beautiful lake, into which falls many a sparkling stream, rushing down amid rocks and tall trees. Would that we were there now instead of toiling over this arid desert. How delightful it would be to plunge into some cool and sheltered pool where no crocodile or hippopotamus could reach us. What draughts of water we would drink," and the black opened his mouth as if to pour some of the longed-for fluid down it.

Sayd imitated the movement of his lips as he translated what was said.

"Chando! Chando!" repeated Ned. "Ask him if he had a father or mother living when he was carried off to become a slave."

"I had a mother, but whether or not she escaped from the slaves I cannot say. I never saw her again. I once had a father, whom I remember well; he used to carry me in his arms, and give me wild grapes and sweet fruit. He was either killed by a lion or an elephant, or was captured by the slave hunters, who, it was said, had been prowling about in the neighbourhood at that time, though they did not venture to attack our village, which was too strong for them."

Ned became very much interested in the account Chando gave of himself. "Inquire whether he can recollect the name of his father."

Sayd put the question.

"Yes, I remember it perfectly well. It was Baraka."

Ned gave a shout of joy, and forgetting his danger and fatigue, and all that was still before him, he rushed forward, and, grasping Chando's hand, exclaimed—

"I know your father; I promised him that I would search for you, and now I have found you. There

can be no mistake about it. He told me that his son's
name was Chando, and you say your father's name
was Baraka, that he disappeared, and has never since
come back. I would far rather have found you than
made my escape, or returned to the coast the possessor
of hundreds of elephants' tusks."

Sayd's exclamations of surprise somewhat interrupted Ned's remarks as he translated them to Chando.
The latter almost let his load drop in his agitation as
he asked, "Is Baraka—is my father still alive? O
my young master, can you take me to him? Can
you find my mother, that we may be together and
be once more happy as we were before he was carried
away to become a slave ? "

" The very thing I wish to do," answered Ned.
" I will try to get your master to give you your freedom at once ; or, if he will not now do so, as soon as
we return to the coast."

So deeply interested were Ned and his companions
in the discovery he had made, that they forgot for a
time their fatigue and their thirst. Even Sambroko
and young Hassan listened eagerly.

" I know where Kamwawi is ! " exclaimed the huge
black. "It is to the north-west, but it would take
many days to reach. It is a fine country, and the
people are brave and warlike ; though the slave
hunters sometimes go there to trap the natives, they
seldom venture to attack the villages."

"It is true, it is true ! " answered Chando. "I

was captured whilst out hunting elephants with some other lads. They all died—I alone lived; and after oeing sold several times became the slave of Abdullah. It was better than being sent away on board a dhow to be carried to some far off land, where I might have been ill-treated by strangers, and have no chance of meeting with any of my own people."

"We must try to reach Kamwawi, and endeavour to ascertain whether Chando's mother is still alive. I promised her husband to bring her back as well as her son if I could find them. It would be a glorious thing to rescue both," exclaimed Ned.

"To do that would be impossible," answered Sayd. "Abdullah will not lead the caravan so far away for such an object. Even should we reach the village you speak of, we should be looked upon as enemies, besides which, the woman is by this time dead, or is married to another husband, and she would not wish to quit her home to go to a distant country for the mere chance of finding her husband alive. You must give up the idea, my friend; the undertaking, I repeat, is impossible."

Ned made no reply, there was too much truth, he feared, in Sayd's remarks. For some time he tramped on, thinking over the matter. At last he again turned to the Arab—

"Sayd," he exclaimed, "I want you to do me a favour—to obtain Chando's liberty. If you have to purchase his freedom, as I suppose you must, I will promise, when we return to the coast, to repay you the cost, whatever it may be."

Sayd smiled at the request.

"Abdullah is not the man willingly to dispose of a healthy slave, who will be able to carry a whole tusk on his shoulders back to the coast," he answered. "Perhaps when the journey is over he may be ready to talk over the matter, but he will demand a high price, of that you may be certain."

"I will pay him any price he may ask. I am sure I shall find friends ready to help me to advance the money until I can send it to them from England."

This answer showed that, although Ned was tramping over the desert in the interior of Africa without a penny in his pocket, or any equivalent in his possession, he had not lost his spirits, and was as sanguine as ever as to getting home some day. As he looked round, however, at the haggard countenances of the Arab leaders and their armed followers, as well as at those of the pagazis, he might with good reason have dreaded that none of them would ever reach the fertile region said to lie beyond the desert. Already many more had fallen, and their track was strewn with the bodies of dead or dying men.

The survivors staggered on, well knowing that to stop was certain destruction. The Arabs no longer attempted to drive them forward, or to distribute the loads of those who sank down among the rest. They themselves were too eager to reach a stream where they might quench their thirst and rest their weary limbs. They would then send back to recover the loads, and pick up any of the men who might still be alive. But hour after hour went by, and the hot sun glared in their faces like the flame from a furnace, almost blinding their eyes. Darkness came on, but still they pushed forward. The same cry resounded from all parts of the caravan : "They must march through the night." Should they halt, how many would be alive in the morning ? Ned had told Chando to keep close to his side, and had supplied him every now and then with a few drops of water. Had others seen this, Ned would have run the risk of having his bottle taken from him. He would, indeed, have been glad to share the water with his companions, but he knew that, divided among many, it would avail them nothing. Not a word was now exchanged among any of Sayd's party, but they kept compactly together. At length Ned caught sight of some objects rising up ahead. They were tall trees with spreading branches. They would not grow thus unless with nourishment from below.

The Arabs and their followers raised a shout, and pressed forward. Every instant they expected to come upon a stream. Several of the trees were passed, and none was seen. At length they reached a bank below which the stars were reflected as in a mirror.

"Water ! water !" was the cry, and Arabs and soldiers and slaves dashing forward, their strength suddenly revived, plunged their faces into the pool, regardless of the danger they ran. Some, more prudent, drank the water from their hands, or from cups they carried, but several, exhausted, fell with their heads below the surface. Some of these were rescued by their comrades, but many were drowned before they could be drawn out. The leaders now issued the order to encamp, and the pagazis, piling their loads, were compelled to search for wood.

On the different bands being mustered by their respective chiefs, nearly half were found missing. Ned set out to search for Chando, and brought him to Sayd's fire to hear more of his adventures, but, though generally talkative, he was scarcely able to utter a word. Directly the scanty meal had been consumed, the weary blacks as well as their masters were asleep. A few hours only were allowed them to rest, when, their strength being somewhat recovered, a large party with water-bottles were sent along the way they had come to the relief of any who might have survived, and to bring in their loads. A few lives were thus saved, and much of the property dropped was recovered.

Sayd had lost several of his men, but he took the matter very coolly, observing " that it was the will of Allah, and could not be avoided."

Heavy as the loss of life had been, the Arabs were still sufficiently numerous to march forward to the rich country where they expected to obtain all their hearts desired. A halt, however, of several days was absolutely necessary to recruit their strength. As Sayd was less fatigued than any of the other chiefs, he undertook to go out hunting in order to obtain food, which was greatly required. Ned offered to accompany him. He took Sambroko, Hassan, and three more of his own followers, and having permission to select any experienced hunters from among the rest of the men, recollecting what Chando had said, he fixed among others on him. All were well armed with muskets, or bows and arrows and spears, and with darts or long knives. Chando, being the most experienced elephant hunter, was sent ahead to look out for game.

The nature of the forest caused the party to become somewhat separated. Ned kept as close as he could to Sayd. Some time had elapsed, when Ned heard a loud trumpeting coming from the forest in front of them.

"T' at's an elephant," shouted Sayd, who was some distance off. "Move carefully forward, and when the creature appears fire steadily, and then spring on one side, but beware lest he sees you, or he may make a rush at you."

Ned resolved to follow this advice. Again they advanced. Ned saw Sayd enter an open glade. He had got but a few yards along it, when a crashing sound from the opposite side was heard, followed by a loud trumpeting. With trunk erect and open mouth a huge elephant dashed out of the cover, catching sight as he came into the open of the Arab. Ned had his gun ready, and, as the animal drew near, steadying his weapon against the trunk of a tree, he fired. The bullet struck the creature, but still it advanced, trumpeting loudly, its rage increased, with its keen eyes fixed on Sayd. The Arab saw it coming, and knowing that, if its progress was not stopped, his destruction was certain, fired at its head, and then, his courage giving way, turned round to fly. Ned gave up his friend for lost. The huge brute would break through all impediments to reach his victim. Just then Ned saw a black form emerging from the wood and springing over the ground at a rate surpassing that of the elephant, against whose thick frontal bone Sayd's bullet had been ineffective. With trunk uplifted the animal had got within ten paces of the Arab, when the black overtook it, a sharp sword in his hand; the weapon flashed for an instant, and descended on the elephant's left hinder leg; then springing on ; ne side the black inflicted another tremendous gash on the right. The monster staggered on, and was about to seize the Arab with its trunk, when, uttering a shriek of pain and baffled rage, down it came with a crash to the earth.

Sayd, stopping in his flight, turned and saw that his deliverer was the pagazi Chando, while Ned at the same moment springing forward congratulated him on his escape. Chando, without speaking, plunged his sword in the neck of the elephant. The rest of the **party on** hearing the firing made their way up to the spot, and complimented Chando on his achievement.

"I am grateful, and must see how I can reward you," said Sayd to the young pagazi.

As meat was much wanted at the camp, the party immediately commenced cutting up the elephant, while messengers were despatched to summon carriers to convey the flesh and tusks. As soon as it was sent off the hunters continued the chase. Ned shot a zebra, which raised him in the estimation of his companions. A giraffe was also seen, and creeping up to it among the long grass the party surrounded it. Before it could escape a bullet from Sayd's gun wounded it in the shoulder, when spears and javelins thrust at it from every side soon ended its life. There was great rejoicing when this meat was brought into camp, and the Arabs and their followers feasting luxuriously forgot their toils and sufferings.

CHAPTER XI.

AGAIN the caravan was on the move. For many days they marched on with varied fortunes, sometimes meeting a friendly reception at the villages they passed, but more frequently being refused admittance, and having to purchase provisions at a high cost, or to pay tribute to the petty chiefs, many of whom, possessing fire-arms, were too formidable to offend. Abdullah declared that they had had enough of fighting, and could not afford to lose more men in unnecessary battles. Hitherto but a small quantity of ivory had been procured, the villagers having disposed of all they possessed to other traders. At this the chiefs were evidently greatly disappointed, and frequent consultations were held among them.

Sayd did not tell Ned the result, but he seemed dissatisfied, and more than once expressed a wish that he had not undertaken the expedition. "But then you would not have found me, and I should not have discovered Chando, so that I am very thankful you came," answered Ned.

Some days after this he observed that they advanced with even more caution than before. Scouts were sent out, who from time to time brought back the intelligence they had obtained.

At length one evening the caravan halted on the confines of a wood through which they had passed. As Ned looked ahead he could distinguish, as the sun set, a large scattered village below them, surrounded by fields and fruit-bearing trees, situated on the borders of a shining lake, a picturesque circle of hills beyond. It was a smiling scene, and spoke of abundance and contentment. Sayd appeared more unhappy than before. Ned again asked him what was about to be done.

"You will see before the night is over," he replied. "My companions have departed from the original intention of our expedition, and I feel much disposed to separate from them, but yet if I do I shall gain no profits, and my friends will have cause to complain."

"Is Abdullah going to trade with the inhabitants of yonder village?" asked Ned.

"No," answered Sayd; "he and the other leaders have devised a plan for acquiring not only all the wealth it contains, but at the same time bearers to convey it to the coast. We have already lost so many pagazis that we shall be unable to transport more than a small portion of what we may purchase."

"Do they, then, intend to attack the village and

make slaves of the unfortunate people ? " asked
Ned.

" It is that they propose to do. It is bad, very
bad," answered Sayd.

" Then let me urge you to take no part in the proceeding," said Ned. "If you cannot prevent them from
committing the crime they contemplate, separate yourself at once from the caravan, take a different route, and
endeavour to obtain the friendship of the natives. I
have heard that they look with respect on Englishmen,
who always treat them justly. I may, therefore, be of
some use to you, as, when they see an Englishman,
they will know that we wish to be at peace, and desire
to deal fairly with them."

" You are right," observed the Arab; " I will
order my people to be prepared for marching in the
direction I may determine on."

Ned was satisfied as far as Sayd was concerned. He
desired also, however, if possible, to prevent Abdullah
from carrying out his infamous project, but how to do
so was the question. An attempt to warn the villagers
of Abdullah's designs would be very difficult. He
could not speak to the Arab leader himself, and Sayd
declared that he had already said all he could to dis-
suade him. He had, therefore, to wait the course of
events. The caravan remained concealed in the wood,
watching the village, until all the lights were extin-
guished and it was supposed that the inhabitants had
gone to rest. In perfect silence the Arabs marshalled

their forces, several of the pagazis being also armed, while the remainder, with a small guard over them, were left in the wood with the goods and provisions.

Sayd, on seeing this, true to his word, drew off his own men, greatly to the anger of Abdullah and the other chiefs. Ned accompanied him, but Chando was obliged to remain in the camp. It was better than being employed in attacking the villagers. Ned was much concerned at having to separate from him. Again he implored Sayd to try by some means or other to obtain Chando's liberty; he received the same answer, "It is impossible."

"Tell him then from me that he must try and join us. He would be perfectly justified in running away if he has the opportunity, and that may occur."

Sayd did as Ned begged him, and then drawing off his men formed a separate camp at a distance from that of Abdullah.

In the meantime the main body of the Arabs, with their armed followers, were creeping down towards the village, keeping concealed among the rocks and shrubs so that they might not be discovered until they were close up to it.

Some time elapsed, when the stillness of night wa broken by the rattle of musketry, followed by the shrieks and cries of the Arabs. The flashes appeared on all sides except that of the lake, showing that the Arabs had almost surrounded the place. Ned could only picture in imagination the cruel deed taking place below him. Presently flames burst forth, now from one part of the village, now from another, until in a short time the whole was in a blaze, while by the ruddy light he could see the dark figures of the inhabitants endeavouring to escape by flight, pursued by their relentless invaders. Still the firing continued, showing that the work of death was going on. At length it ceased. After some time a large mass of people could be seen by the light of the flames, while the Arabs were distinguished rushing here and there, lance in hand, driving their frightened prisoners before them. The cruel act had been accomplished; upwards of a hundred of the villagers had been captured, and the Arabs, exulting in their victory, returned to their camp. Ned accompanied Sayd, who desired to have a parting interview with Abdullah. As they approached the camp they saw the prisoners, men, women, and children, sitting on the ground, the armed guards standing round them, while the remainder of the Arabs' followers were employed in forming forked poles to place on the necks of the* refractory, and in preparing the ropes by which the others were to be bound together.

The meeting between Sayd and his former leader was more stormy than might have been supposed, the latter abusing him in no measured terms for his desertion, and threatened his destruction and that of his followers should he try to proceed through the country. To attempt to obtain Chando's liberty under these circumstances would have been useless. Sayd and Ned therefore returned to their own camp. Ned did his utmost to keep up Sayd's spirits, pointing out to him that he had acted rightly and would have no cause to repent his decision, though he himself was bitterly disappointed at having to leave Chando, whom he had hoped some day to restore to his father.

"In what direction do you propose to proceed?" he inquired of Sayd.

Having consulted Sambroko: "I intend to march northward and then to turn to the east. He tells me that we pass near many villages inhabited by elephant hunters, who are sure to have a good supply of ivory; and as the Arabs have not gone through that part of the country for a long time, we shall obtain it at a moderate price, besides which, the people are likely to prove friendly."

At daybreak Sayd's small caravan commenced its march, Sambroko uttering a farewell shout to their late companions, who replied by derisive cries. "They may shriek as they like," he observed, "but they will before long change their tone. They will either have to recross the desert, or will have to go a long way round to avoid it, when they will find enemies in all directions through whom they will have to fight their way."

Ned would have rejoiced at getting free of Abdullah had Chando been with him, though he did not despair

of recovering the young slave on his return to Zanzibar. Still he knew that many circumstances might
prevent this. Chando might succumb to the fatigues
of the journey, as many others had done, or might be
killed should the caravan be attacked by hostile
natives, or Abdullah might ship him off with other
slaves on board a dhow, should they reach the coast.
All Ned could do, therefore, was to hope that none of
these events would occur.

There was but little time for thought. Sayd was
anxious, by forced marches, to get away from the
neighbourhood of the village which had been so
treacherously treated, lest the inhabitants of other
villages—supposing that he and his followers had
been engaged in the proceeding—should attack them
and revenge themselves on his head. They marched
on therefore all day, with only a short halt to take
some food, water being abundant and the tall trees
protecting them from the hot sun. At night they
encamped under a gigantic sycamore, the boughs of
which would have shaded twice their number from
the rays of the sun. Near it was a stream from
which fresh water could be procured, and Sayd would
gladly have halted here some days had not Sambroko
advised that they should push on.

At daybreak they were again on the march. They
had, however, to supply themselves with food, but so
plentiful was the game that the hunters had not to go
far out of their way to obtain it. Sambroko, who

was their chief hunter, succeeded in killing a zebra, which afforded meat to the whole party, and the next day, whilst stalking at the head of the party, he brought down a magnificent giraffe, which he managed to surprise before the animal had taken alarm. It was of the greatest importance to reach a village, which Sambroko said must be passed before the news of the Arab raid could get there, and at length it came in sight, standing on a knoll surrounded by palisades, above which the roofs of the houses could be seen.

As they approached, Sambroko set up a cheerful song announcing that friends were drawing near and desired peace. The result was anxiously watched for. Should the gates remain closed, the caravan would have to pass by as far as possible from the village with the prospect of being attacked in the rear. Greatly to their satisfaction, however, Sambroko's song produced a favourable effect, and the villagers came out shouting a welcome.

Sayd thought it wise, however, not to enter, but gave notice that he had brought goods with which to purchase ivory and provisions. An active barter was soon going forward. Eight tusks were procured and an ample supply of provisions. Sayd also obtained information from the natives that several villages were situated in the direction he wished to go, the inhabitants of which were likely to prove hostile. They offered to furnish guides who would conduct his

party through the jungle to a distance from them.
This offer he gladly accepted, confident that no
treachery was intended. After a short rest the
caravan again moved forward. The carriers marched
in single file, the path not allowing two to walk
abreast.

Sayd and Ned, accompanied by Hassan, led, Sambroko bringing up the rear, the other armed men
being equally distributed in the line, while the two
guides kept ahead. The party were soon buried in
the depths of the forest. Perfect silence was preserved. Now they emerged into a more open country
and pushed forward with rapid steps. As darkness
was coming on, there was little risk of being seen
from a distance. Led by their guides they continued
through the early part of the night until another
forest was reached, where they lay down to rest, no
fires being lighted, no sounds being uttered. The
guards kept a strict watch lest a lion might
spring out on the slumbering party. Before dawn
they were again on foot and moving forward as
on the previous evening. For three days they thus
advanced, until the guides assured them that they
might continue to the eastward without fear of
molestation until they reached the village of
Kamwawi.

"You must be cautious how you approach it,"
they observed; "the people are brave and warlike,
and if they think you come as enemies they will be

sure to attack you, but if they consider you are friends they will treat you with kindness and hospitality."

"Kamwawi!" exclaimed Ned, when he heard the name; "that surely is the village to which Chando told us he belonged?"

"Yes, but there are others with similar names, so that we can never be certain," answered Sayd. "I find that the one spoken of is four days' journey from hence, and as we must camp to procure food it may be longer than that before we reach it."

The provisions held out another day after they had parted from their friendly guides, and they had now only their own judgment to depend upon. Once more they were encamped. No human habitations were visible, no signs of cultivation. The country around appeared to be deserted. They would have, however, in consequence a better chance of meeting with game, and Sambroko promised that he would bring enough food to feed the whole party for several days. Ned offered to accompany him, but Sayd was too tired after his morning march to leave the camp. Hassan and another freed man followed, carrying spare guns. It was difficult to say beforehand what game might be met with, whether elephants, or buffaloes, or giraffes, or zebras, or deer, but the hunters were prepared for any one of them. Sambroko declared that all game were alike to him, that he knew their ways and habits. Ned, however, was the first to shoot a deer, which they came upon

suddenly before the animal had time to fly. While
the blacks were employed in cutting it up, Ned walked
on ahead in the hopes of finding some large game.
Feeling confident that he might easily make his way
back to the camp again he crept cautiously on, looking to the right hand and to the left, and endeavouring to peer over the bushes in front. At length he
saw some dark objects moving up and down above the
tops of the branches directly in front of him. He
crept on and on ; getting a little closer he saw that
they were elephant's ears. Ambitious of shooting the
true monarch of the wilds, Ned, regardless of the
danger he was running, crept on, hoping to plant a
bullet in a vital part of the animal before he was discovered. He had got within twenty yards of the huge
creature, when he stepped on a rotten branch, which
broke beneath his foot. The noise warned the elephant that an enemy was near. Up went its trunk.
It began breaking through the intervening brushwood. Ned, retaining his presence of mind, stood
watching until he could get a fair shot, intending
then to follow the advice which Sayd had before
given. The head and shoulders of the animal came
in sight. Now was the moment to fire; he pulled
the trigger. Without waiting even to see the effect
of his shot, for had he remained where he was he
would the next instant, should it have failed to take
effect, have been crushed to death, springing on
one side he ran for shelter behind a tree which he

had just before noted. The elephant, with trunk uplifted, broke through the brushwood, trumpeting loudly
in its rage. Looking about and not seeing its enemy
it stopped short. Ned in the meantime re-loaded as
fast as he could, and stepped out to fire again. The
quick eye of the elephant detected him. To fly was
now impossible ; he must bring down the creature, or
run a fearful risk of being caught. He fired, when
the elephant rushed towards him with extended trunk.
Ned saw that the branch of a tree hung just within
reach above his head. By a desperate effort, which
under other circumstances he could scarcely have
made, he swung himself up on to the bough, and ran,
as a sailor alone can run, along it until he reached
the stem, up which he began to climb with the rapidity
of a squirrel. The elephant had, however, seen him ;
even now he was scarcely beyond the reach of its
trunk, which, looking down, he saw extended towards
his feet. In vain he tried to spring up to the nearest
branch. He felt the end of the creature's trunk touching his legs ; should they once be encircled he would
be drawn hopelessly down. He involuntarily uttered
a loud shriek, and endeavoured to draw up his feet.
It was answered by a shout from Sambroko and the
other blacks ; at the same instant he heard a shot.
The elephant's trunk was no longer touching him, but
the exertion he had made was beyond his strength ; his
hands relaxed their hold, he felt himself falling. Con-
sciousness, however, did not desert him. He expected

in another instant to be crushed to death by the creature's feet, or to be dashed by its trunk against a
tree. He fell heavily to the ground. All he could
see for a moment was a dark form above him. He
made a desperate effort to struggle out of its way, but
his limbs refused to aid him. He closed his eyes,
resigned to his fate. But the death he expected did
not come. A shout sounded on his ear. Looking up
he saw the black stooping over him, while a few paces
off, lay the elephant which Sambroko's shot had
brought to the ground.

"Well done, young master, well done!" cried the
black. "You are not much hurt. We will carry you
to the camp, and send the people to bring in the meat
and tusks. We shall have fine feasting, and all will
be grateful to you for having supplied us with meat."
Such was what Ned understood the black to say.

He was very thankful to find himself placed on a
litter, composed of a couple of poles and some cross
pieces cut down from the neighbouring trees, when
his bearers immediately set off towards the camp.
The men, on hearing of their success, uttered shouts
of joy, while half their number set off to bring in the
tusks and elephant meat and venison. Sayd attended to Ned's hurts. One of his ankles was severely
injured by his fall, and his shoulder was also sprained.
It was evident that he would be unable to march for
several days.

"You must remain here until you have recovered

your strength," said Sayd. "The people will be in no hurry to move while they have such an abundance of meat. If you cannot walk after a few days, they must carry you, and they will be ready to do so, as they owe their feasting to you. Sambroko tells me that one, if not both, of your shots mortally wounded the elephant, though it was his which saved your life, for had he not fired the moment he did you would probably have been destroyed by the beast."

"I am very thankful to him, at all events," said Ned; "but I am very sorry to detain you when it is so important to push forward."

"Allah wills it, we must not repine," answered Sayd; "and as we have to remain, we must lose no time in fortifying our camp to protect ourselves against wild beasts as well as human foes."

In accordance with this intention he ordered his men to cut down stakes and to collect a large quantity of prickly pear-bushes which grew in the neighbourhood. A square fence was then formed with stakes, the interstices being filled up by masses of bushes, making it perfectly impervious, so that even elephants would hesitate before attempting to break through it. Within the circle rude huts were built for the accommodation of the garrison, one of which, of rather better construction, was devoted to Ned's use. He had hardly taken possession of it when he felt a painful sensation come over him, and he was conscious that he was attacked by fever. Fearful fancies filled his brain, hideous forms were constantly flitting before him, while during his lucid moments he endured the greatest depression of spirits. He gave up all hope of ever again seeing those he loved or his native land. Hour after hour he lay racked with pain. Sayd sat up by his side, continuing to assert that he would recover. Still not only hours but days and weeks went by, and he heard Sayd acknowledge to Sambroko that he feared the young master would die after all. The very next day, however, Ned felt himself better, though too weak to walk. Sayd had hitherto borne the delay patiently, but he now again became anxious to proceed. Sambroko, though at first successful, had of late shot but a small quantity of game.

At length Sayd ordered a litter to be formed, and directed four of the pagazis to carry Ned, giving their packs to others, who grumbled greatly at the increased weight of their loads. Sambroko having fortunately killed an eland, the people were restored to good-humour, and consented the next morning to commence the march.

Again the little caravan moved on, and as the men had been well fed they made good progress. About an hour before sunset they once more prepared to camp, a spot near a thick wood having been selected, with a stream flowing at no great distance. Ned had been placed on the ground, and the people were scattered about collecting branches for huts and fuel for

their fires, when suddenly loud cries burst from the
forest, and a band of fierce-looking savages, armed
with spears and javelins, burst out from among the
trees. The men had left their arms in the centre of
the spot chosen for their camp ; near them lay Ned
on his litter, with Sayd seated by his side. The
young Arab immediately rose, and lifting his rifle,
pointed it at the foremost of the savages. A fight
appeared imminent. Should Sayd or Sambroko fire,
the next instant the blacks would be upon them, and
the rest of the party, having only their axes or
knives, could offer but a feeble resistance. The in-
truders held their ground in spite of the warning
shouts of Sayd and Sambroko. Ned, unwilling to
die without attempting to strike a blow, was crawling
towards the arms to possess himself of a musket,
when one of the savages raised his spear to dart at
him. At that instant a shout was heard proceeding
from the forest, out of which Ned saw a person rushing without weapons in his hands. The black who
was about to hurl the spear hesitated, and the next
instant Ned recognised Chando, who, coming forward,
turned round and addressed his countrymen, for they
were of his tribe, signing also to Sayd and Sambroko
to lower their weapons. The savages, who just before appeared bent on the destruction of the travellers,
now advanced, uttering expressions of good-will and
welcome.

Seeing peace established, Chando knelt down by

Ned's side, pouring out expressions of joy at having found him, and inquiring anxiously the cause of his being unable to walk. Sayd replied, and then eagerly asked how he himself happened to arrive at so fortunate a moment. As Sayd listened to the account Chando was giving him his countenance expressed deep concern.

"What has happened ?" asked Ned, when the black at length ceased.

"What I am not surprised to hear," answered Sayd. "Abdullah had proceeded but three days' journey with his newly-captured slaves, and some sixty tusks or more which he had obtained, when a large force of negroes, who were lying in ambush, burst out on the caravan. The Arabs and some of their followers fought bravely, and, with a portion of their slaves and pagazis, escaped to a height where their enemies dared not follow them; but the remainder of the carriers threw down their loads and tried to escape through the forest. Some were killed, but Chando, with a few others, got free, and came on in this direction, till they fell in with a hunting-party of his own tribe, from whom he learned that an attack was to be made on a small caravan, which he at once conjectured was ours. Hastening on, he arrived just in time to prevent a fight, which would probably have ended in our destruction."

Chando nodded his head and smiled as Sayd was speaking. He appeared to have another matter, to speak about which he evidently considered of the greatest importance. He at once communicated it to Sayd.

" What does he say ? " asked Ned.

" That his mother is alive and one of the most important people in Kamwawi. That her brother is the chief, which is a fortunate circumstance, as he undertakes that we shall be received in a friendly way and escorted by his people as far as the influence of their tribe extends."

The two parties encamped together, the hunters bringing in an ample supply of venison and elephant flesh. The next morning they proceeded towards Kamwawi. Ned had now no longer any difficulty in obtaining pagazis, each of Chando's friends wishing to have the honour of carrying him. In two days they reached Kamwawi. Messengers having gone ahead to announce their coming, the gates were thrown open, and the villagers streamed forth to welcome them, headed by their chief; near him walked a woman, superior in appearance to the other females of the party. No sooner did Chando see her than he rushed forward and threw himself at her feet. She lifted him up, embraced him, bursting into tears. She was his mother—Masika. At length, when released from her arms, the chief welcomed him in almost as affectionate a manner.

The whole party were then received in the usual native fashion, and Sayd, without hesitation, accepted the chief's invitation to remain at the village as long as he might desire.

Great was Masika's astonishment at hearing tha.
her husband was alive, though she hesitated about
accepting Ned's offer to take her and Chando to
England.   She bestowed, however, every care on her
white guest, and contributed much by her skill to
restore him to health.

Whenever she and her son could get Sayd to
interpret for them, they would come and sit by Ned's
couch, listening eagerly to the accounts he gave them
of Baraka, as well as to the adventures he himself had
met with.

" Wonderful, wonderful ! "   exclaimed   Masika.
" Chando says he must accompany the young master,
and I will go also. I will find my husband and bring
him back; he will be a great man here. He has
become so wise, so good ! "

Masika at last made up her mind to undertake the
expedition, and occupied herself in making such preparations as she considered necessary. It was some
time, however, before Ned recovered the use of his
feet, and could walk about without pain. The fever,
too, had left him very weak. He was thankful for
the rest he obtained. Sayd now became anxious to
proceed, though his followers were in no hurry to
leave their present quarters. He had purchased a
large number of tusks from the villagers, and had
engaged a dozen of them to assist in conveying his
property to the coast. He had, indeed, by honest
commerce made a far more profitable expedition than,

in all probability, had Abdullah, even though he should succeed in reaching the coast with his captured slaves.

During the stay of the caravan at Kamwawi, Chando and a number of people, excited by the prospect of selling their ivory at a good price, several times went out hunting and succeeded in bringing in six elephant tusks, and four from the jaws of hippopotami, which they had slain.

After a stay of several weeks, the caravan, considerably increased in size, marched forth from the gates of the village with colours flying, drums beating, horns sounding, and people shouting their farewells and good wishes. Ned felt in better spirits than he had done for a long time, as he was once more able to march alongside Sayd, Chando, who was now not only a freed man, but was looked upon as a person of considerable consequence, being generally in their company. Masika, carried in a sort of litter by four bearers, followed close behind them.

They had a long journey before them, and many dangers and difficulties to encounter. Sayd confessed to Ned that his stock of ammunition had run very low, and that should they encounter an enemy they might be unable to defend themselves. They hoped, however, to find the natives friendly, and that they should march forward without interruption.

He had still retained a sufficient amount of goods to purchase provisions and to pay the usual tribute to

the chiefs through whose territory they would have to
pass. Sayd issued strict orders to his people to
expend none of their powder and shot unless in a
case of absolute necessity.

Day after day they marched on, sometimes being
received as friends, at others finding the gates of the
villages closed against them, especially when they
reached the districts through which the Arab caravans
had passed. Still, they were two hundred miles or
more from the coast. Fifteen miles was the very
utmost length they could perform in one day's journey,
and generally they did not get through more than ten
miles. Thus, with the necessary halts for hunting or
purchasing provisions, and the detention they might
meet with from chiefs, it would still take them three
weeks before they could reach the coast.

Three weeks, after so many months spent in the
interior, seemed nothing to Ned, and he would not
allow himself to think of the many other delays which
might occur. They had rivers to ford, swamps to
cross, dense forests to penetrate, and occasionally a
desert region to get over, on which occasions, in spite
of the heat of the sun beating down on their heads,
they pushed forward as fast as they could move.
Once they ran short of provisions, but a successful
hunt the following day restored the spirits of the
party. When game could not be procured they
obtained supplies of honey from the wild bees in the
forests, as well as fruits of various descriptions, in-

cluding an abundance of grapes from the vines, which grew in unrestrained luxuriance along the borders of the forest, forming graceful festoons on the projecting branches of the trees.

From the character they had received of the natives they had reason to expect an unfriendly reception from the inhabitants. They did their best to avoid these villages; or, when compelled to pass near, Sayd, without hesitation, paid the "honga," or tribute demanded. The people, however, generally treated them in a friendly way on observing that they had no slaves, no chains, or men with forked sticks to their necks, and Sayd explained that their mission was peaceable, their object being to carry on a fair trade. There appeared, indeed, every prospect of a satisfactory termination of their journey.

They had encamped earlier than usual one day in order to allow Sambroko, Chando, and the other hunters to go out in search of game. In the meantime huts were built, wood collected, and fires were lighted to be ready for cooking it. They were expecting the return of the hunters, when Sambroko and Chando were seen rushing at headlong speed towards the camp, where they arrived almost breathless, exclaiming—

" To arms! to arms! The enemy are upon us. No time to lose; before many minutes they will be here. We saw thém coming in this direction."

Sayd, on further questioning the two hunters, was

convinced that their report was true. To encounter a horde of savages on the open ground on which they were encamped would be dangerous; but near at hand was a knoll with trees on its summit, which Ned had observed. He advised Sayd to retreat to this spot, as they might there, should they be attacked, defend themselves with greater hope of success. The pagazis shouldering their loads, the cooks snatching up their pots and pans, and the armed men their guns, the caravan beat a hurried retreat and quickly ascended to the top of the knoll. Ned, on surveying it, advised that a breastwork should be thrown up with such trees and bushes as could be quickly cut down, and which would enable them to defend themselves against any enemies destitute of fire-arms. Every man, therefore, capable of using an axe was set to work, and several tall trees being brought down were piled one above another on the most accessible side of the knoll. Where the ground was soft stakes were driven in, and in other places thick branches were heaped up, so that in a short time a breastwork was formed calculated greatly to strengthen their position. The people were still labouring at it, when from out of the forest to the north issued a band of warriors with long spears in their right hands and shields on their arms, their heads bedecked with zebra manes, above which waved plumes of ostrich or eagle feathers, while their robes of skin, as they rushed on, streamed behind them. Rings were round their legs, to which bells were suspended as they ran. On either side of the main body were skirmishers. They shouted and shrieked vehemently, and flourished their weapons as if to inspire terror in the hearts of those they were about to attack. On they came, fresh bodies appearing until they might have been counted by hundreds. Ned watched them with no small anxiety.

If determined to conquer at the sacrifice of life, they could not fail to succeed; but he had seen enough of black warriors to know that when met with determination they were not likely to persevere. Sayd seemed to be of the same opinion. He spoke to his people, and urged them to fight to the last. Masika also addressed her followers, reminding them of their character for courage, and urging them to fight bravely in defence of their white friends, and of her and her son. The men responded with loud cheers, which were heard by their advancing foes. It had the effect of making the latter halt just as they came within gunshot, when the chiefs, who were known by their tall plumes and the leopard skins round their waists, were seen speaking to their followers, apparently urging them to the attack.

" Would that we had the means of letting them understand that we have no wish to injure them, and desire only peaceably to pass through their country," observed Sayd.

" Haven't we got something to serve as a flag of

truce ? " asked Ned. " A piece of white calico at the end of a spear would answer the purpose."

" They would not understand it," answered the Arab.

" I should like to try," said Ned.

" You would probably be speared as soon as you approached."

Scarcely had he spoken when once more, with loud shrieks and cries, the warriors came on.

" Fire, my brave men ! " cried Sayd, and every gun was discharged, Sambroko picking out one of the chiefs, who fell wounded, as did several more, though none were killed. Still other chiefs led the way; undaunted they advanced in spite of another volley, the defenders of the knoll loading and discharging their muskets as fast as they could. In vain Ned set them the example, and Sayd urged them to take better aim. Except Sambroko and a few of the more disciplined men, they fired at random.

Their assailants had almost reached the foot of the knoll when some of Sayd's men cried out that their ammunition was expended and asked for more. In vain Hassan was sent to look for it. Package after package was turned over, but none was to be found. Three or four rounds at the utmost remained in the pouches of any of the party; when they were expended there would be nothing but the breastwork to stop the progress of their foes. Sayd entreated those who had cartridges not to throw a shot away. On the enemy pressed; they had begun to climb the side of the knoll, hurling their javelins at its defenders. Sayd, in spite of the desperate state of affairs, exhibited the coolest courage, his fire checking several times the advance of the foe; but he and Ned had both discharged their last round. The chief leading the way had almost gained the breastwork, when Sambroko, leaping over it, dealt him a blow on the head with his clubbed musket, which sent him falling back among his followers. Others, however, were rushing on to avenge his death.

In another instant they would have been up to the breastwork, when a loud shout was heard and a body of men, bearing an English ensign in their midst, was seen emerging from the wood to the south-east. As they advanced a British cheer was heard, which was replied to by Ned, and echoed, though in a somewhat strange fashion, by his companions, who, picking up the javelins aimed at them, hurled them back on their foes. The latter seeing a fresh body approaching to the assistance of those they were attacking, and dismayed by the fall of their chief, retreated hastily down the knoll, and on reaching level ground took to flight to avoid a volley fired at them by the new-comers. On came the British party. Ned, with his heart leaping into his mouth, rushed down the hill to meet them. In another instant his hand was being grasped by Lieutenant Hanson and his old messmate Charley Meadows, while Tom

Baraka, springing forward, clasped him in his arms, exclaiming—

"O Massa Ned, we find you at last! I always said dat you 'live. Hurrah! hurrah! Now him tink him die happy."

"Don't talk about dying," said Ned, "for I have found some one else whom you will rejoice to see, and I will tell you all about it presently; but I want to know first about my uncle and Aunt Sally and Mary?"

"Dey all well, an' de lieutenant he off dis berry coast in fine schooner which bring us here."

Lieutenant Hanson and Charley then explained more fully what had occurred. How they had come out in the "Hope," and how they had heard from an Arab, one of the few belonging to Abdullah's caravan who had escaped, that a young Englishman answering Ned's description was up the country, and was very unlikely ever to find his way down to the coast. They had accordingly hired the most trustworthy men they could obtain, and set off without delay to his rescue.

"And very thankful we are to find you," exclaimed Mr. Hanson.

"You could not have arrived more opportunely, for never since I have been in Africa have I been in so great a danger of losing my life; and now I want to break the news I have to communicate to my faithful friend Tom Baraka," said Ned.

In the meantime Chando, prompted by curiosity to

look at the white men, had descended the hill. Ned seeing him, took his hand and led him up to Baraka.

"Tom," he said, "I promised to find your son if I could. What do you think of this young man? Are you ready to acknowledge him as your little boy Chando?"

Tom gazed into Chando's face for a few seconds, then grasping his hands, he rapidly uttered a few words which Ned could not understand. The young black replied, and the next instant they were clasped in an affectionate embrace. Tom's paternal feelings assured him that he had found his long lost boy, but a still greater surprise was in store for him. In another minute he and Chando were rushing up the hill together. Ned and his friends followed, and were just in time to see the meeting between Tom and his wife. Though so many years had passed away since he had parted from her, he appeared to know her immediately, and if he exhibited his feelings in a more exuberant manner than a white man might have done, they were not the less affectionate and genuine.

Ned introduced Sayd, expressing his gratitude for the protection he had received. Mr. Hanson and Charley at once recognised him as the young Arab who had been saved from the sinking dhow. It was necessary now to arrange what was to be done next. The two parties agreed to camp together on the knoll, and resolved to proceed to the coast by the route Mr. Hanson and his people had followed, thus avoiding the savage warriors who had just been defeated, and who would undoubtedly seek for an opportunity of revenging themselves. An important point, however, had to be settled. Would Tom return with his son to Kamwawi, or would they accompany the English back to the coast ?

" Me lub him wife, him son too; but him lub Massa Pack, an' Baraka's heart break if he not say good-bye. And Missie Sally an' Missie Mary ! Oh ! what shall him do, what shall him do ? "

Tom had some difficulty, it appeared, in persuading his wife and Chando to proceed to the coast, but the descriptions he gave of the wonders they would see overcame their objections. Still, Chando expressed the not unreasonable fear that he might be seized by Abdullah and carried off again into slavery, and very nearly turned the scale the other way. Mr. Hanson, however, through Sayd, promised him protection, and his mother's fears on that score were quieted.

The two parties now united forming a strong body, marched through the country without opposition, except from the natural difficulties which presented themselves.

The " Hope " was found at anchor in the harbour, where Lieutenant Pack had promised to wait for the expedition, having returned there the previous day.

His joy at recovering his nephew may be supposed

Sayd, who had expected to be obliged to carry his ivory to Zanzibar, was delighted to find that Mr. Pack was ready to purchase the whole of it at a far higher price than he could have expected to have obtained at that market. Leaving his people encamped under the command of Sambroko and Hassan, he accepted an invitation to return on board the "Hope" to Zanzibar to purchase fresh stores for another expedition, and he promised Ned that he would not only never again have anything to do with slave-trading, but, after the experience he had gained, would keep aloof from all those who engaged in that barbarous traffic. Tom Baraka, his wife, and Chando also came on board, Tom having inspired Masika with a curiosity to see the wonders of the island, as Zanzibar is called. The great desire of his heart was accomplished. From the commencement of the journey he had instructed her in that faith which had afforded him support and comfort during his long exile from the home he had expected never again to see. Though she did not at first understand all Tom said, her mind, as well as that of her son, became gradually enlightened, and he had the happiness of seeing them both baptized before they left Zanzibar under the escort of Sayd, who undertook to protect them and to restore them safely to their native village. It cost Tom, however, much to part from his old master and Ned, though he was reconciled to the separation by the belief which they had taken care to instil into him,

that he might prove an unspeakable blessing to his
countrymen by imparting to them the truths of the
Gospel and instructing them in the arts of civilisa-
tion.   He and Sayd were the last persons to quit the
"Hope," as, with a full cargo of ivory and other
African produce, she sailed for England.

Though the voyage was long, Ned had scarcely
finished the account of his adventures when the
schooner reached the Thames, and the two lieutenants,
richer men than they had ever before been in their
lives, accompanied by Ned and Charley, set off to
report to Mr. Farrance the success of their undertaking.   On reaching the house they were greatly
surprised at hearing that he, with his brother, had
a few days before started for Triton Cottage.

On this Lieutenant Pack, bidding farewell to Mr.
Hanson, accompanied by Ned and Charley, immediately set off for home.   As they approached, Ned,
looking out of the carriage window, saw a young lady
leaning on the arm of a gentleman who bore a strong
resemblance to Mr. Farrance.   It needed not a
second glance to convince him that the young lady,
though much taller than the Mary he remembered,
was Mary herself, and calling the post-boy to stop, in
a moment he was out of the chaise and running
towards them.

" It is—it is Ned ! " cried Mary, and forgetting her
advanced age, and many other things besides, she
threw her arms round his neck and burst into tears; but

as she looked up directly afterwards and saw Lieutenant
Pack coming stumping eagerly towards them, the
bright smile which overspread her countenance showed
that they were tears of joy. The lieutenant took her in
his arms and kissed her cheek again and again.

" How is sister Sally—all right I hope?"

" She is at home with Uncle Farrance; and here is
my papa," she added, pointing to a gentleman standing near her.

" Your papa, Mary?" exclaimed the lieutenant
putting out his hand. "I am happy to see you, sir,
whatever claim you have to that relationship, although
you shall not carry off our Mary if I can help it."

The gentleman smiled faintly. " You certainly,
sir, have a superior, if not a prior claim, from all the
loving-kindness which you and your sister have shown
her, and I should indeed be ungrateful were I to act
contrary to your wishes," answered the stranger.

" Well, well, come along, we will settle that by-and-
by," said the lieutenant, as he walked hurriedly on.
I want to see my good sister Sally and assure
her that I am as sound in health and limb as when I
went away." He had let go Mary's hand, and she
and Ned now followed, Charley having got out some
time before to take a shorter cut to the coast-guard
station, where he expected to find his father.

Miss Sally did not go into hysterics, as Mary had so
nearly done, on seeing the lieutenant and her nephew,
but received them both as her affectionate nature

prompted, though as she looked up into Ned's face she declared that, had not he come back with his uncle, she would have had some doubts as to his identity.

Mr. Farrance now came forward and more formally introduced his brother, assuring the lieutenant of the proofs he had obtained to his entire satisfaction that he was Mary's father, "though," he added, as he took him aside, "I fear, from the trials and sufferings he has endured, his days on earth are destined to be few."

This, indeed, when the lieutenant had an opportunity of observing the elder Mr. Farrance, he thought likely to be the case. The lieutenant and Ned were too much engaged—the one in describing his voyage, and the other his adventures in Africa—to inquire after any of their neighbours, though it was very evident that Miss Sally had a matter of importance which she wished to communicate.

"Come, Sally, what is it?" exclaimed the lieutenant. "Has Mrs. Jones got twins? or is Miss Simpkins married? or is poor old Shank dead and not left enough to bury him, as I always said would be the case?"

"Hush, hush," said Miss Sally, looking towards Mary and her father, who, with Ned, were seated at the window. "It is about Mr. Shank I wish to tell you. The old man is dead, and it was partly about his affairs that Mr. Farrance came down here, or they would have sent for Mary and me to London.

It is a very extraordinary story. He was once a miser, and although suffering apparently from poverty, had no less than thirty thousand pounds, which he has left to our dear Mary. He did so before he knew he was her grandfather, which he turns out without doubt to have been. His only daughter married Mr. Farrance, and was lost in the Indian seas on board the ship from which you saved Mary and Tom. Mary was with the old man until his death, and was a great comfort to him, but she had not the slightest suspicion that he intended to leave her a sixpence. From what our friend Mr. Thorpe had said, however, I was not so much surprised as I might otherwise have been. Mary had so interested him in the sufferings of the Africans, caused by the slave trade, that he left a note expressing his hope that she would employ such means as she might have at her disposal to better their condition, especially by the establishment of missions, which he expressed his belief would prove the best way for accomplishing that end."

No one would have supposed from Mary's manner that she had suddenly become an heiress. Indeed no one was more astonished than Ned when he heard the account Miss Sally had given his uncle. It seemed, indeed, to afford him much less satisfaction than might have been supposed. Her wealth, however, was not increased by her father's death, which occurred a short time afterwards.

Several years passed away; by that time Africa had

been explored by the many energetic travellers **who** have so greatly benefited its people by acting **as** pioneers to the missionaries who have since gone forth to carry to them the blessings of the Gospel.

Mary had to wait until she was of age before she inherited her grandfather's property, when she became the wife of honest Ned Garth, then a commander, and who, greatly to his surprise, found that Mr. Farrance had settled on him a sum equal to her fortune.

Mary did not forget Mr. Shank's wishes, nor did Ned the scenes he had witnessed in Africa, both ever showing a warm interest in its dark-skinned races by contributing liberally towards the support of every enterprise for their benefit.

THE END.

LONDON:
PRINTED BY JAS TRUSCOTT AND SON,
Suffolk Lane, City.

www.ingramcontent.com/pod-product-compliance
Lightning Source LLC
Chambersburg PA
CBHW031344020726
47499CB00005B/1393